Virtual Museums – A Plea

FORUM VIRTUELLE MUSEEN

VIRTUAL MUSEUMS

– A PLEA –

**AROUND THE CLOCK.
AROUND THE WORLD.**

Deutscher Kunstverlag

AVICOM

d|u|p

AVICOM
ICOM
international committee
for audiovisual, new technologies
and social media

Cover image: Rüdiger Kern after a design by
by Karl-Ludwig Döring with the help of Canva
Typesetting: Rüdiger Kern, Berlin
Printing and binding: CPI Books GmbH, Leck

ISBN 978-3-422-80238-4
e-ISBN (PDF) 978-3-422-80237-7
DOI **https://doi.org/10.1515/9783422802377**

Library of Congress Control Number: 2024944666

Die Deutsche Nationalbibliothek lists this publication in the Deutsche Nationalbibliografie; detailed bibliographic data are available at **http://dnb.dnb.de**.

Deutscher Kunstverlag
Part of Walter de Gruyter GmbH
Berlin Boston
d|u|p düsseldorf university press
An Imprint of Walter de Gruyter GmbH
Berlin Boston

This book is published with open access at
www.deutscherkunstverlag.de
www.degruyter.com
dup.degruyter.com

MIX
Papier | Fördert gute Waldnutzung
FSC® C083411

Encouraging the establishment and illustrating the characteristics, requirements and opportunities of virtual museums

TABLE OF CONTENTS

FOREWORD

September 1890: In a newspaper advertisement in Bonn, impresario Neumann announces his "world-famous Museum of Anatomy, Ethnology, and Natural Sciences" for the fair in (Bonn-)Pützchen. The audience will be able to marvel at "All operations, all diseases" in the show booth, as well as the "Penetration power of the new, small-calibre jacketed bullets of the repeating rifle model 88 on 5 soldiers standing in a row" and "Anatomical dissections every half hour." Neumanns Panoptikum is just one of many sideshows that, in a time when museums are still temples of learning for the educated, adopt the designation "museum" to attract the masses.

As long as there have been museums, there have also been museums that are not museums – if subjected to the criteria of the new museum definition recently adopted after much debate by the world's most significant museum umbrella organisation, ICOM. "Museum" is what its operator considers to be a museum – or its visitors. This remains true to this day in the physical museum world. It not only concerns many local history museums and vintage car exhibitions, even though both resemble more of a storeroom, but also many discovery museums that offer spectacular media installations and hands-on activities but not a single original object.

The fact that the term "museum" is by no means protected to the annoyance of museum associations and museum professionals is also evident, perhaps even more so, in the digital world. Here, it becomes particularly evident how much there is a lack of precise definition, of a set of criteria. If a physical museum, conforming to ICOM's definition, labels its conglomerate of digitally presented offerings – from a virtual tour through the depot or selected objects of its special exhibition to an interactive history adventure for kids in a museum escape room – as a "Digital Museum", then it is far from it.

What it is, when it makes sense, whether as a complement to a physical museum presence or as a necessary alternative – that is what this book deals with. It offers much more than a set of criteria. It is rather an extensively unfolding initial contribution to the discussion, almost a handbook, as has not been available before. AVICOM, the ICOM International Committee for Audiovisual, New Technologies and Social Media, has been critically observing and evaluating the developments in digital museums since its founding in the early 1990s, primarily in a still predominantly analogue era, providing recommendations, bringing together museums and producers as well as museum professionals and students alike. AVICOM considers the exchange and cooperation with the "Forum Virtuelle Museen" working group, with the "Art Education and Cultural Management" program at Heinrich Heine University Düsseldorf (Dr. Julia Römhild and Prof. Dr. Bernd Günter), as well as with the ICOM Young Professionals as professional enrichment for the museum media world. Thus, AVICOM is also happy to support research and studies on media and digital museum management, as is exemplary taught and practiced at Heinrich Heine University in Düsseldorf. The results published in this book are certainly looking forward to engaging in discussions with the museum scene on various points. However, one thing is for sure, they fulfil a need and point the way.

Dr. Michael H. Faber
President of ICOM AVICOM

FOREWORD BY THE AUTHORS

Ten years ago, when three of the authors involved in this document contemplated the idea of a virtual museum on a topic for which there was no physical museum, it was impossible to find support for the plan to establish such a museum, despite intensive efforts and the demonstration that a virtual museum can and should fulfill all the core tasks of the ICOM task taxonomy. Gradually, the idea emerged that it was necessary to disseminate the concept of a "virtual museum" more widely and to contribute to discussions within the museum community and cultural management.

The extended author group "Forum Virtuelle Museen" now presents a discussion paper intended to promote conceptual discussions, but perhaps also to develop empirically feasible designs for virtual museums. This raises two fundamental questions: "What is a virtual museum or what is virtual about a museum concept?" and "For which topics or configurations can a virtual museum be particularly suitable?" A brief, pragmatic – if somewhat vague – answer is provided to the first question. Comprehensive answers, accompanied by many examples and addressing issues to which traditional, non-virtual museums cannot provide sufficient answers, are provided to the second question.

It is not surprising that at the end of 2023, the media reported that UNESCO, along with other international institutions, was planning to establish a **virtual museum for stolen cultural artifacts**[1]. Among other considerations, this report demonstrates the need to initiate a more intense discussion about virtual museums, especially given the enormous progress made in digitization in recent years, and the possibility that discussions on this topic can now be more open and constructive.

The author group welcomes every contribution to the relevant discussion and every support of the concepts, especially from museum associations, cultural and educational institutions, and the media. We are particularly grateful for the opportunity to present conference papers at a conference organized by ICOM AVICOM and the University of St. Andrews (Scotland) in September 2023, specifically to Dr. Kamila Oles and Dr. Michael H. Faber. The present publication is supported by the International Committee AVICOM of the museum association ICOM. ICOM Germany, through its president, Dr. Felicia Sternfeld, stated: "The board of ICOM Germany thanks the author group 'Forum Virtuelle Museen' for the well-founded scientific and equally accessible elaboration of current concepts and discussion states surrounding virtual museums. We see this as a multifaceted contribution to the development of digitality in museums, which will have a lasting impact on the international museum world." The German Museums Association, through its board and

1 **https://core.unesco.org/en/project/505GLO4000** [accessed on 13 June 2024].

managing director David Vuillaume, expressed its support as follows: "The German Museums Association welcomes the publication as an entry point and stimulus for discussion on the topic. The association notes that the topic is continuously evolving, and developments are so rapid that it probably requires a different format to be able to respond more current and provide suggestions for the future. Nevertheless, the association regards this look into the history of digitization as a valuable basis for understanding the present." We are also very grateful to the ICOM Germany Young Professionals, who "support the discussion on virtual museums initiated by the plea and want to continue it within our network. We look forward to the exchange on this." A big thank you also goes to our constant encourager and critical supporter Prof. Dr. Hans-Martin Hinz (President ICOM 2010–2016), to whom we are grateful for many inspirations. We are indebted to Dr. Christian Gries for valuable critical remarks.

This publication was made possible by the Open Access Fund of Heinrich Heine University Düsseldorf. Additionally, our thanks go to de Gruyter/Düsseldorf University Press, especially to Dr. Anne Sokoll, who accompanied us through the publication process and provided assistance throughout. We thank Anne Seebeck and Karl-Ludwig Döring at Heinrich Heine University Düsseldorf for their editorial assistance.

Düsseldorf, August 2024
The author group "Forum Virtuelle Museen"

REINHARD GRÖNE

THOUGHTS ON THE INTRODUCTION

The message of this publication is: Establish virtual museums! Where analogue museums are lacking or topics are less suitable for analogue museum work, where added value such as "available everywhere and at any time" is desired: Create virtual museums! But virtual museums that function like analogue museums and according to standards of the International Council of Museums (ICOM)[1]!

Digitalisation and virtual worlds are increasingly permeating the cultural sector and the creative industries. When it is difficult for cultural offerings to find their audience, they can or must actively reach out to their audience. This also applies to museums, which can find and retain audiences in different ways and with different formats. Even a virtual museum is fundamentally a museum. Especially if it not only complies with the "ICOM Standards for Museums" and above all the museum definition adopted by the International Council of Museums in Prague in 2022, but also fulfils all the standards of the German Museums Association and ICOM Germany. The "Standards for Museums" are intended as guidelines, as a kind of "guard rail" for museum work and museum tasks. The respective characteristics and weighting vary from museum to museum and are essentially derived from the objectives of the museum founders and operators. Initially, this has nothing to do with analogue versus digital and offline versus online. Both analogue and virtual museums fulfil the current ICOM definition[2] in equal measure:

> A museum is a not-for-profit, permanent institution in the service of society that researches, collects, conserves, interprets and exhibits tangible and intangible heritage. Open to the public, accessible and inclusive, museums foster diversity and sustainability. They operate and communicate ethically, professionally and with the participation of communities, offering varied experiences for education, enjoyment, reflection and knowledge sharing. (ICOM 2022)

Only the requirement for a suitable museum building that is available in the long term could give rise to a need for discussion. Seen in the light of day, a museum location made

1 The International Council of Museums (ICOM) was founded in 1946. The General Secretariat is in Paris. ICOM has around 50,000 members in around 140 countries. Link to the homepage of the International Network: **https://icom.museum/en/**.

2 Following a participatory process lasting several years, the original definition was revised and the new museum definition was adopted at the ICOM General Conference in Prague in August 2022.

of bits and bytes on the World Wide Web fulfils some of the other requirements even better than a building made of marble, stone and/or concrete.

According to ICOM, it is essentially about the tasks of researching, collecting, preserving, exhibiting, interpreting and mediating. Virtual museums that exist exclusively online do this just as well or just as badly as the classic buildings made of marble, stone and concrete in the analogue, "offline world", with their content and operators. Hybrid versions *additionally* utilize the other reality: the tried and tested offline museums use digital media and the internet to complement their work and use them where they are efficient and effective. A purely virtual museum also endeavours to make an appearance in the offline world. In addition to marketing-driven aspects, this is also to be able to offer something to the digitally neglected senses: Haptics, taste, smell, shared reception experiences. And finally: just as there are pop-up stores, there can and will also be pop-up museums.

In principle, the establishment of a virtual museum should be seriously considered if there appears to be no equivalent in the analogue offline world for a relevant topic. The following are four further, different reasons for setting up a purely virtual museum. These motives are further specified in the third chapter.

Economic arguments

The financial and economic aspect will often play a decisive role: A museum of local history "built" on the Internet from bits and bytes, such as that of the Erkelenzer Lande ("Virtual Museum Erkelenz"), has arisen from the realisation that there are no funds available for a museum building in the foreseeable future. Nevertheless, the collected artefacts and their scientific processing and the associated research need a "home", a "location" where the interested public can find and view them.

A virtual museum is much more cost-effective than its analogue counterpart, both in terms of construction costs and ongoing operating costs. Thanks to home office, personnel and infrastructure costs are also different. This further applies to the numerous freelancers, without whom no museum operation can be attractive and customer-orientated (user- or visitor-orientated).

Ecological arguments

Sustainability assessment and evaluation is also becoming increasingly important. If the construction and operation of an analogue offline museum ties up more resources and leaves a larger carbon footprint than the construction and operation of an online cultural offering, then there is at least a need for examination and discussion.

Conceptual arguments

There are topics that are much more difficult to present and process in the analogue world than in the virtual world. These include phenomena such as *time, lost art and cultural treasures, lost landscapes and the future.* Also there are all kinds of philosophical areas, from *changing values* and *capitalism* to the topic of *persecuted or annihilated minorities,* and of course *climate change and its effects* through to *politics, power, freedom and dictatorship.* Or the *origin of life* and the *theory of relativity.*

Almost everywhere where artefacts are only "aids" for approaching a phenomenon: *money* – *clocks* – or are only available as mostly digital placeholders: *Looted art* or the *Green Vault*. Or *virtual water* and *cryptocurrency.*

User-orientated arguments

"The digital visitor is just as important to us as the visitor on site." (C. Paul, Technoseum Mannheim, 2019 in a guest lecture at the University of Düsseldorf). The digital visitor can access a virtual museum at any time and any place – without travelling. They can possibly contribute their own content and research the content and engage in discourse at any time. Accessibility, availability, sustainability and (physical) accessibility – apart from language barriers – can therefore be arguments in favour of visiting and engaging with virtual museums from the user's point of view, in addition to the content.

Societal and social arguments

Further arguments can be found in social interaction, which can be given a new dimension through virtual museums: The use of newer technologies in the field of social XR, which combine elements of augmented reality and virtual reality with the social sphere, can also enable and promote social interaction in the virtual space. Cross-border meetings with friends, acquaintances and colleagues become possible in order to create shared museum experiences. Live events such as parties, conferences and exhibition openings with larger groups of users can also be realized as meeting points in virtual museums using social XR and offer the opportunity to overcome digital isolation and also integrate the "fun of social interaction".

ISABELLE BECKER AND THERESA STÄRK

1. ON THE TERMINOLOGY OF THE VIRTUAL MUSEUM

1.1 Current debates on a definitional approach

What constitutes a virtual museum? In the current discourse on the subject or concept of the "virtual museum", which began in museum studies as early as the 1990s, the term is used excessively, vaguely and for various museum phenomena (cf. Niewerth, 2020, p. 526; Schweibenz 2016, p. 198). The attempt at a definitional approximation is made more difficult by the fact that the individual phenomena that generally bear the (self-chosen) term "virtual museum" (can) differ greatly from one another and it is sometimes difficult to distinguish them from digital libraries or databases (cf. Schweibenz 2016, p. 198). In addition, the term is not uncontroversial: there are numerous alternative terms that can mean the same thing, but do not necessarily have to. While terms such as *electronic museum* and *digital museum* focus on the technicality of museum operations or the discrete functioning of digitality, terms such as *online museum*, *cyberspace museum* or *web museum are* more pragmatic and descriptive (cf. Niewerth 2020, p. 526; Schweibenz 2001, p. 6). However, the term "virtual museum" has become widely accepted since the 1990s (cf. Schweibenz 2008, p. 132 et al.) and is also the basis of this publication.

The debate about virtual museums began in the late 1990s at the latest with the establishment of the World Wide Web and the associated private use of the Internet. While computer technology has been used in museums since the 1960s, both internally (especially in collection management) and externally (especially in exhibition design), the idea of a museum whose exhibitions are purely digital is now being discussed in the wake of rapid mass media developments (cf. Niewerth, 2020, pp. 526–527). An early definition of the virtual museum was published online as early as 1996 by the Encyclopaedia Britannica (cf. Niewerth 2018, p. 126), which, however, denies virtual museums (still unchanged today) the uniqueness and permanence of analogue museums:

> [...] a collection of digitally recorded images, sound files, text documents, and other data of historical, scientific, or cultural interest that are accessed through electronic media. A virtual museum does not house actual objects and therefore lacks the permanence and unique qualities of a museum in the institutional definition of the term. (Britannica Online, n.d.)

The exclusivity of virtual museums, which solely house and exhibit digital objects and data, is emphasized and clearly differentiated from the museum in its institutional form of existence with *"real objects"* (*"actual objects"*).

The International Council of Museums (ICOM) has not yet defined the term virtual museum and has refrained from providing its own definition (see ICOM Germany 2010 and the lack of references to this topic in the run-up to the General Conference 2022).

The term "virtual museum" varies in the research literature: sometimes it stands for a digital presence of all collections on the web, sometimes it describes only those presentations of digital collections that are detached from a specific institution and have no underlying collection of their own.

1.2 Virtual museums as a hybrid extension of the classic museum

As Schweibenz (2016) explains, virtual museums can be understood in two main ways: on the one hand as an exclusively digital concept and thus separate from the analogue world or without an analogue counterpart, and on the other hand as an extension or supplement to a real museum; a position which, according to Schweibenz, has meanwhile assumed the more dominant position (p. 198).

Following this approach and according to the understanding of the authors of this treatise, virtual museums constitute equivalent, digital alternatives to physical museums in the metaverse as "institutions in their own right" (Schweibenz 2019, p. 7). Virtual museums should also be accessible to the public (possibly for a corresponding entrance fee) and use interactive elements to educate, research, exhibit and create an experience for visitors (cf. Hermon/Hazan, 2013). This publication defines the virtual museum as a virtual representation of a collection in its final form, which can have a material or virtual origin. Objects of such an autonomous virtual museum can be born-digital objects (such as net art, video art and video game art) as well as originally material objects that are reproduced online as digital copies.

Hybrid forms of the virtual museum, such as online collections or digital exhibitions, which can be categorized as a classic analogue museum and are treated as an extension of such a museum into the digital space, should initially be distinguished from these purely virtual museums without physical representation. As mentioned above, these hybrid forms appear to be of overriding importance in practice to date, as from the perspective of existing museums, the function of virtual museums as an instrument for expanding physical museums takes centre stage. Nevertheless, a different interpretation of the term is also noticeable here: On the one hand, virtual museums are seen as "representations" of the physical and transfer this into the digital world. On the other hand, virtual museums can also be "real" extensions that also fulfil other functions and exhibit other objects than the physical museum – and thus have a certain autonomy and their own (organisational) structure – for example as a "digital branch" or "digital division" of an existing museum.

1.3 Virtual museums as an exclusive digital exhibition space

The platform for virtual museums Virtual Multimodal Museum (ViMM, URL: **https://www.vimm.eu**) defines virtual museums as digital entities that use the characteristics of a museum to supplement and expand the museum through personalisation and interactivity as well as content. The virtual museum is contrasted here with the physical museum (cf. Polycarpou 2018).

As a permanent counterpart to online exhibitions, virtual museums can exist independently of a physically present location. Objects are reproduced digitally or presented and made accessible exclusively in virtual space as "born digital objects".

This plea is primarily aimed at those virtual museums that represent a "genuine extension" or "independent branch" of a physical museum and, in particular, those that function completely autonomously and independently of actual museums as "institutions in their own right".

2. STATUS QUO: MUSEUM TASKS AND VIRTUAL MUSEUMS

2.1 Museum definition and tasks

(BERND GÜNTER)

Since 1986, the International Council of Museums (ICOM) has standardized and further developed the concept of the museum within the framework of the Code of Ethics for Museums. In addition to a new definition of "museum" in 2022, which is reproduced and commented on in the introduction, a kind of short definition was already established in 2007 – probably for pragmatic reasons – which summarizes the characteristics of museum work remuneratively on the basis of the five museum tasks and which is also taken into account in the revised definition. According to this definition, a museum fulfils five tasks:

- *Research*
- *Collect*
- *Preserve*
- *Interpret*[1]
- *Exhibit*

This taxonomy, which can also be understood as normative, has apparently also proven to be capable of achieving international consensus. In the debate on the definition of museums at ICOM, which has been raging since around 2011, the task-based definition appears to form a minimum consensus. The version of the taxonomy currently under discussion has become part of the proposed new version. Incidentally, one can speculate whether the change in order is motivated by cultural policy, if the new ICOM museum definition 2022 puts the task of "research" in first place.

If one accepts this enumeration of tasks, the question of completeness or appropriate additions arises. One suggestion made by this author since 2011 is to take into account the fact that a museum fulfils the task of a "competence centre" for its chosen topic. In the 2022 museum definition, the task of "knowledge sharing" comes very close to this. In this sense, a museum is a point of contact for topics, exhibits, etc. A virtual museum can also do this or precisely this, if necessary with a kind of editorial office.

1 The English verb "interprets" in the new version of the 2022 museum definition replaces the "communicates" originally used in the 2007 version. For this manuscript, however, the term "communicate" is retained (see chapter 12).

2.2 Considerations on changes to the museum's tasks (JULIA RÖMHILD)

The digitisation – or: virtualisation of museums – can make an important contribution to fulfilling the museum tasks defined by ICOM in the metaverse. However, it also influences the tasks, develops them further and requires changes in dealing with cultural heritage and related, further-reaching issues.

For virtual museums, the changes in the range of tasks involved in *researching, acquiring or collecting and preserving* are recognisable in the following areas, for example:

- *Changing collections* (chapter 9): In addition to digitised analogue exhibits – which always require the analogue counterparts to be stored – the creation and use of new, purely digital exhibits without a corresponding physical counterpart is conceivable and is already being practised: purely digital art is already being created in the form of videos, objects, non-fungible tokens (NFTs), VR worlds and games. Incidentally, the v-must-project has highlighted the possibilities of preserving and making available intangible artefacts in virtual museums. Artificial intelligence (AI) is also playing an increasingly important role in the production and creation of images and works of art (e.g. the portrait of Edmond de Belamy, see also 16.3) – although the creative work is (still) carried out by humans (e.g. with the help of OpenAI's DALL-E software).
- *Change in archival services:* Analogue exhibits can be archived in digitised form and displayed worldwide. The state of the art makes non-invasive interval scanning possible, which allows even more data to be collected about works of visual art and reproduced in detail online. Digital, networked online archives are conceivable, taking into account appropriate (internationally valid) keywording – for example using keywording projects such as ARTigo or Google Art Project. 3D printers also enable the (re)translation of digitised or digital exhibits into a physical form – for example for illustrative purposes or for temporary pop-up museums.
- *Change in research* (Chapter 8): Digital inventories and digital collection management with corresponding indexing also make networking in research easier and offer opportunities for virtual museums to position and establish themselves as "hubs" of networks or as centres of expertise for their respective topics.

Opportunities for virtual museums in dealing with the public and special target groups are also becoming clear in the area of museum *exhibitions* and *communication:*

- *Change in curation and transfer of knowledge:* Curating exhibitions can change. In virtual museums, for example, it is conceivable that exhibitions could be put together collaboratively by visitors using a crowdsourcing approach – or even customised exhibitions tailored precisely to the visitor's preferences. The type of knowledge sharing can also possibly follow this approach: Digital outreach programmes – provided they are integrative and interesting enough – can also generate attention among those who do not otherwise visit museums. Accordingly, there are also opportunities in the area of *audience development* – the acquisition and retention of new target groups: the fact that access in virtual space is independent of time and place harbours great potential for reaching different (non-)visitor groups (see also section 4.1). One aspect that should also be mentioned in the context of curation and knowledge sharing is the use of artificial intelligence. Projects such as the federally funded **CHiM – Chatbots in Museums**[2] show initial approaches to using artificial intelligence for art and cultural education.

- *Change in communication with target groups:* Whether for analogue or purely virtual museums, budget deficits can make digital communication channels appear advantageous. The use of social media, for example, not only offers potential advantages in terms of reach, networking and audio-visual presentation, but also makes it possible to get to know the digital audience in a cost-saving and relatively uncomplicated way by means of social media monitoring. Tools such as Instagram, Tik-Tok etc. are usually relatively inexpensive (although not free), but usually require a relatively high time budget and expertise in terms of storytelling and content management. It should be borne in mind that communication takes place "at eye level" and around the clock, and that it may well be beyond the control of the operating institution.

The above-mentioned trends certainly do not represent a comprehensive list, but they do show the first starting points and opportunities for virtual museums in the interpretation of "classic" museum tasks[3] .

2.3 Considerations of changes through the use of artificial intelligence

(REINHARD GRÖNE AND JULIA RÖMHILD)

Furthermore, the use of artificial intelligence will continue to increase in all areas of life in the coming years, including museums. For this reason, the understanding of AI used here should be briefly outlined at this point. While definitions vary, the definition of the High-Level Expert Group (HLEG) formed by the European Commission on the topic of artificial intelligence can be referred to here.[4] Key characteristics of AI can be summarized as follows: the perception of sensory impressions of the environment, information processing and interpretation, autonomous decision-making and adaptation to a certain degree (= "learning"

2 **https://www.interaktive-technologien.de/projekte/chim** [accessed on 13 June 2024].

3 For further information, see Deutscher Museumsbund e.V. (2019): Guide to working professionally in museums, Berlin.

4 "Artificial intelligence (AI) systems are software (and possibly also hardware) systems designed by humans(2) that, given a complex goal, act in the physical or digital dimension by perceiving their environment through data acquisition, interpreting the collected structured or unstructured data, reasoning on the knowledge, or processing the information, derived from this data and deciding the best action(s) to take to achieve the given goal. […]" (HLEG 2019)

from experience) and the achievement of specific, predefined goals (see Samoili et al. 2020). However, the areas of application of AI in museums are certainly initially in the field of so-called "weak AI" – i.e. far removed from machine learning and sentient intelligence (= "strong AI") – and thus rather in the area of algorithmic decision-making and support for humans in certain tasks. Murphy et al. (2022) show practical examples in the field of museum applications in the form of commentary analyses, the calculation of occupancy forecasts, automatic speech recognition and adaptation of object texts, the preparation of collection data using machine learning methods, etc. and refer to AI tools such as IBM Watson, Google Cloud and Microsoft Azure.

The rapid development of artificial intelligence capabilities therefore has an impact on all types of museums, both analogue and virtual. With AI support, analogue museums can introduce completely new and very complex aspects into exhibitions and research (cf. Thiel and Bernhard 2023). By posing appropriate questions to AI, ideas and areas will be opened up that in the current museum world build on the knowledge and skills of the staff involved. AI expands this scope by further dimensions; its knowledge and suggestions become increasingly complex and extensive simply through its application. A powerful tool that will provide museum staff with more and more new suggestions for their work.

This is basically the same in the virtual museum. But there is another crucial aspect. If the AI is also available for use by visitors, friends and patrons as part of the virtual museum, their museum-related thematic knowledge will grow even deeper and even faster: in addition, aspects of culturally very different questions will be answered and their results incorporated. All of this can be quickly realised and made visible in the everyday life of the virtual museum. The virtual museum becomes an interactive and democratic place.

2.4 Reports on "new" digitally orientated museums

(ANJA KIRCHER-KANNEMANN)

In recent years, numerous digital presences have emerged that operate under the term "virtual museum". What almost all of these offerings have in common is that they are nearly indistinguishable from a website or online collection. They present collections of digitised artefacts and archive materials, sometimes with additional information.

Most of these digital offerings do not fulfil the criteria for a virtual museum, which this publication is based on, as they do not have their own digital or (partially) physical collection. However, this is one of the cornerstones of a museum.

The digital offerings can be roughly divided into four categories:

1. Digital offerings that draw on existing digital collections from other museums, archives or other cultural institutions and process them under special aspects and themes. Examples:

Original Names (with links)

- **Google Arts and Culture**
- **Europeana**
- **Deutsche Digitale Bibliothek**
- **Kulturerbe Niedersachsen**
- **Museum digital**
- **Museum-digital Thüringen**
- **Digitale Kunsthalle ZDF**

Translation

- Google Arts and Culture
- Europeana
- German Digital Library
- Cultural Heritage Lower Saxony
- Museum digital
- Museum Digital Thuringia
- Digital Art Gallery ZDF

2. Digital offerings based on an analogue or partly digital collection that are made visible in digital space in the absence of an analogue space. Examples:

Original Names (with links)

- **Virtuelles Migrationsmuseum**
- **Barnums American Museum**
- **CIA Museum**
- **Virtuelles Museum Digital Humanities**
- **Virtuelles Museum Erkelenz**
- **Virtuelles Grimm-Museum**
- **Virtuelles Straßenbahnmuseum Chemnitz**
- **Haller ZeitRäume**
- **Virtuelles Museum FC St. Pauli**
- **Virtuelles Fastnachtsmuseum**
- **Virtuelles Nikon-Museum**
- **„Die Jeckes" – Ein virtuelles Museum**
- **Virtuelles Stadtmuseum Winnenden**
- **Virtuelles Museum der Wissenschaft**
- **Virtuelles Museum Kultur macht Potsdam**
- **Virtuelles Obstbaumuseum Rheinland**
- **Virtuelles Heimatmuseum Thomas-berg**
- **Virtual Museum of Caribbean Migration and Memory**

Translation

- Virtual Migration Museum
- Barnum's American Museum
- CIA Museum
- Virtual Museum Digital Humanities
- Virtual Museum Erkelenz
- Virtual Grimm Museum
- Chemnitz Virtual Tram Museum
- Haller ZeitRäume
- Virtual Museum FC St. Pauli
- Virtual carnival museum
- Virtual Nikon Museum
- "The Jeckes" – A virtual museum
- Virtual City Museum Winnenden
- Virtual Museum of Science
- Virtual Museum Culture makes Potsdam
- Virtual Fruit Tree Museum Rhineland
- Virtual museum of local history Thomasberg
- Virtual Museum of Caribbean Migration and Memory

3. Digital offerings that represent an extension of analogue museums and/or archives. Examples:

Original Names (with links)	Translation
• Das Herzog Anton Ulrich Museum Braunschweig bietet ein **virtuelles Kupferstichkabinett** und ein **Münzkabinett**	• The Herzog Anton Ulrich Museum Braunschweig offers a virtual cabinet of engravings and a coin cabinet
• **Virtuelles Antikenmuseum Göttingen**	• Virtual Museum of Antiquities Göttingen
• **Literaturarchiv Saar-Lor-Lux-Elsass**	• Saar-Lor-Lux-Alsace Literary Archive
• **Zeiss-Archiv**	• Zeiss archive
• **Synagoge Niederzissen**	• Niederzissen Synagogue
• **Virtuelles Museum für Kinder und Jugendliche**	• Virtual museum for children and young people
• **Virtuelles Museum Trambahn**	• Virtual Tram Museum
• **Virtuelles Museum für Naturschutz**	• Virtual museum for nature conservation
• **Virtuelles Brückenhofmuseum**	• Virtual Brückenhof Museum
• **Museum of the World (British Museum)**	• Museum of the World (British Museum)
• **Dreams of Dali**	• Dreams of Dali
• **Anne Frank – Das Hinterhaus**	• Anne Frank – The Secret Annex
• **eMuseum: Himmelswege**	• eMuseum: Heavenly paths
• **West Highland Museum**	• West Highland Museum
• **Kommunikation Nürnberg**	• Communication Nuremberg
• **Museum für Kommunikation Berlin**	• Museum of Communication Berlin

4. Digital offerings that have no analogue reference and have exclusively digital representation (metaverse). Examples:

- **DFC Francisco Carolinum** the "first museum for NFT art in the metaverse"
- **Area for virtual Art**
- **Musee Dezentral**

5. "v-must": a first EU project

From 2011 to 2014, an EU-funded *Virtual Museum Transnational Network* ("**v-must**") project focussed on the topic of "virtual museums". However, the project focused on identifying the framework conditions for (future) virtual museums and the concept and implications of virtuality. A glossary and key criteria for virtual museums were developed.

3. SUITABILITY CRITERIA OR "WHAT MAKES SENSE AS A VIRTUELL MUSEUM?"

As already discussed, a virtual museum satisfies the task-oriented definition of a museum set out in the "Code of Ethics" of the International Council of Museums (ICOM): researching, collecting, preserving, exhibiting and communicating – all in one organisational unit.

The following list shows important characteristics that "analogue" museums do not have or that have specific effects on the Internet or in the digital world that go beyond the usual effects of museum work.

Features of a virtual museum:

- Virtual = medium, no physical counterpart; yet possibly: combination of analogue and digital elements
- Aggregation of content from the areas of tangible and intangible cultural heritage
- Possibility to create new contextual connections
- Virtual, digital presentation and storage (theoretically unlimited); rapid customisation and modification
- Preservation of analogue objects, exhibitions and presentations (digitised; backup motif)
- Utilisation of current web-based IT technologies
- Multimedia character
- Ubiquity; worldwide access with very low barriers (especially language); universal participation
- Change and possibly expansion of the space of perception and experience
- Conservation of various resources used in analogue museums; contribution to sustainability
- Global networking of museum content and resources
- Expanded and simplified research options
- Possibility of fast, individualised interaction with very low barriers
- User participation/interaction and active co-design options – limited by curating
- Immediate feedback and analysis of visitor/user behaviour
- Possibility of digital creation (new objects, new interpretations, new discussions, "new worlds")
- Sustainability arguments, e.g. when dispensing with paper and printing, energy aspects
- Educational function and comprehensive competence centre

- Compatibility with ICOM standards (museum objectives and functions; Code of Ethics)

Some of these characteristics also apply to analogue museums, but may have a different weight and different implications in a virtual museum.

The following theses identify possible suitability criteria for virtual museums. They provide a preliminary answer to the question: In which situations and for which problem solutions can the establishment of a virtual museum be considered?

Virtual museums are suitable for *content and topics*:

1. For which analogue museums do not yet exist
2. Which are abstract and/or intangible, e. g. for the topic of time
3. With a focus on international research interests, networking and co-creation
4. With a focus on web and digital art: digital collections, exhibitions with digital exhibits; digital "re-composition"
5. With a focus on objects and cultural heritage that have been destroyed and/or lost ("lost art")
6. With a historical focus and for the reconstruction of historical places, their surroundings and contemporary documents in the form of images and simulations based on historical, archaeological and palaeontological facts and documents – accessibility is particularly beneficial here.

Virtual museums are also suitable for the following *problem situations and educational tasks:*

7. A (planned) museum does not own a building for its objects, collections, exhibitions etc. and is unlikely to be able to build or own one in the foreseeable future (e. g. the Erkelenzer Lande local history museum ("Virtual Museum Erkelenz").
8. An existing museum has no scope for expansion – except into the digital space.
9. The aim of a museum is to present a complete collection and all available material and exhibits, including those from the depot.
10. A museum tries to reach visitors and other stakeholders (e. g. researchers, media and others) everywhere, worldwide and at any time.
11. A museum endeavours to enable complementary perspectives on themes and objects that are not physically possible.
12. Exhibits and exhibitions may not or cannot be physically presented for conservation or security reasons. This also includes securing endangered objects, especially in the event of war.
13. There is a lack of an "experimental space" for experiments in the field of curation, mediation and collection, for example in the field of digital art (such as the NRW Forum, which awards "digital residencies" or the Musee Central with a temporary exhibition of digital art).

14. There is a lack of training, teaching and learning venues for students, volunteers and professionals in further education who digitally curate exhibitions and thus "practise" curatorial and mediating practice. Virtual museums can thus create practice scenarios, just as simulations are used as learning experiences in medical training, mechanical engineering, electrical engineering and many other fields.
15. Topics and content should be presented that have the potential and intention to develop further with co-creation by visitors – which can be easier to implement online or via links with social media than in analogue space.

4. TARGET GROUPS AND CUSTOMER BENEFITS

4.1 Define target groups

(REINHARD GRÖNE AND JULIA RÖMHILD)

Target and interest groups ("stakeholders") include all addressees who are also "players" in analogue museums. The above-mentioned ubiquity offers a special opportunity for expansion. Stakeholders are all persons, groups of persons and institutions who are interested in an issue, are affected by it and may (be able to) make claims against it. In the following, we will take a brief look at what is probably the most important stakeholder group: the visitors or users.

In principle, the usual analogue museum audience is conceivable as *users* for virtual museums: this is already very diverse in itself. Approaches to visitor typology are helpful here, such as John Falk's typology (2009), which divides visitors into *Explorers, Professionals, Facilitators, Experience Seekers* and *Rechargers* based on their motivation to visit.

Based on this categorisation, Stender and Stärk (2022) derive digital user profiles in their **Art 4.0 toolbox**[1] that take into account the specific characteristics of the digital audience:

- *Entertainment users* who "visit" digital collections to discover something new and be entertained.
- *Professional users* who are professionally connected to the cultural sector and are specifically looking for information for use in a professional context.
- *Hobby users* who specifically seek to gain knowledge in their leisure time and want to learn something on their own initiative.
- *Creative professionals* looking for specialised information, free-choice learning options or (freely) usable image material.
- *Cultural tourists* who would like to prepare or follow up an analogue museum visit.
- *Commercial users* as a special group who are only interested in high-resolution image material for further use.

In addition, target groups can also be categorised online according to the intensity of use, depending on whether they

- Consume information and content passively, i.e. only "read along" ("*passive users*"),

1 **https://www.kuk.hhu.de/curriculum-40-nrw-digitale-kunstvermittlung-art-40** [accessed on 13 June 2024].

- are connected to the institutions via their own profiles and thus also receive information (*"online connectors"*),
- Collect and tag information (*"online collectors"*),
- comment on contributions and actively participate in the exchange (*"online contributors"*) or
- Create their own content as *prosumers* and create user-generated content (*"creators of online content"*).

The decisive factor here is that for *audience development* – the acquisition and development of new target groups – virtualisation appears to make it possible to break down (analogue) barriers: virtual spaces allow distances of all kinds to be overcome: in terms of location, time and also socially. Cultural participation can sometimes be better facilitated in this way, as additional target groups can be reached ("outreach"), for example:

- Music, video streaming and podcast users as well as gamers in their role as entertainment users[2], including so-called "educationally disadvantaged" groups.
- People interested in specific topics as professional users or hobby users who are not looking for cultural diversion, but for knowledge about a specific (niche) topic.
- Children and young people who can be introduced to virtual museums through school programmes in the field of media education and thus the educational institutions and teachers themselves who would like to offer such programmes.

However, a prerequisite for successful target group identification and addressing (market segmentation) and thus for successful audience development is ideally prior and accompanying audience and user research, which deals with questions such as:

- Who is interested in the selected topic?
- How do I reach the audience (better: an audience segment)?
- What expectations does the audience have? Of the content? Of the educational services? For additional services?
- What are the possible motives or barriers for visiting or not visiting?

In the case of "shareholders" as a further subgroup of stakeholders, two types of shareholders are culturally relevant (although there are also mixed forms such as "private-public partnerships"):

- *Public-law shareholders: Publicly* funded and operated institutions established under public law – usually active in education/mediation or cultural preservation.
- *Private shareholders* with two different intentions:

2 For more information on media use in an intermedia comparison and the motives for use in Germany, see ARD/ZDF: Study on mass communication 2021, **https://www.ard-zdf-massenkommunikation.de** [accessed on 14 January 2024].

- Socio-political positioning of the shareholder (patronage, Corporate Social Responsibility, Corporate Citizenship)
- Self-supporting as a competence centre (incl. consulting & sales)

Both "shareholder" types are not primarily orientated towards profit. This fulfils the requirement of the current Prague ICOM definition proposal "not for profit". The same applies to the requirement for a "permanent institution" – it makes no difference whether the museum invites visitors in the online or offline world. The new ICOM definition is forward-looking on these points – which is important because otherwise it will not be recognised as a "museum" – which could mean a decisive loss of impact.

4.2 Define multipliers

(REINHARD GRÖNE)

Possible multipliers for a virtual museum are as diverse as the topics that are made accessible in a virtual museum. They can be found in the circle of precisely those *stakeholders* who belong to the thematic environment of the museum. In principle, they differ little from the multipliers who also support an analogue museum in its public perception. The support of multipliers is required for various tasks in the ongoing operation of a virtual museum. However, they are particularly needed when the museum is put into operation in order to draw the attention of their *peer groups* to the (new) virtual museum.

The weighting of multipliers is sometimes very different. And the effort that multipliers have to put in is usually much lower in the digital world. Once content and messages of all kinds have been produced, they can be duplicated and shared at the touch of a button without much effort. And they can be easily distributed on communication channels that already exist and are already being used under the sender's own name.

Among the multipliers the initiators and *operators of* the virtual museum should be mentioned first and foremost. As in the analogue world, they have a substantial, sometimes intrinsic interest in ensuring that *their* topic attracts as many visitors as possible and/or achieves a high level of visibility. Sufficient visitor numbers are the prerequisite for the sustainable economic operation of any museum. Regardless of whether it is *public*, *private* or a mixture of the two. The currency "visitor" remains. In the digital universe, it is the "clicks" (e. g. page impressions, unique visitors) that are needed and are considered one of the possible parameters for success. A virtual museum without clicks will at some point be just as much at risk as a "visitorless" museum in the analogue world.

Other interested multipliers are the interest groups associated with the respective topic areas. Organisations and associations that want to promote *their* topic. The prerequisite for this is that suitable content, eye-catching messages and invitations are available, which can be easily processed and forwarded due to their digital nature. Provided with direct links to the respective museum, they also position the association as a competent source of information. In this way, they lead to a resilient win-win situation for everyone involved in the process.

But it is not only the themed associations that can position themselves in the best possible way; the museum world itself can also position itself in a contemporary and future-orientated way. If the work that virtual museums also do fulfil the current museum requirements of national and international museum associations, they too can place themselves at the forefront of digital development. The advantages of digital duplicability also apply here.

In the same way, supporters and sponsors of virtual museum activities are able to share their support with their own customers directly and without any effort on their part. A multiplier effect that contributes to their own brand – but at the same time can also attract potential interested parties to the virtual museum and its work.

Bloggers and *influencers* can also easily jump on this bandwagon. If the virtual museum has exciting content to tell, they will use this *storytelling* for the relevance of their own channels and to generate more *followers*. Because here, too, clicks are the decisive currency. Bloggers and influencers naturally also make themselves interesting for museum sponsors.

Museum visitors themselves can also easily become interested ambassadors in their neighbourhood. Original offers, which can also be customised for distribution in social media, make the word-of-mouth propaganda of the analogue world much more effective thanks to the easy-to-use digital distribution: the visitors themselves become interesting for their friends and followers.

And if the virtual museum also initiates, builds and maintains its own community with attractive and popular "gimmicks", similar to crowdfunding campaigns, then this quickly pays off in additional clicks. Such community building also includes a museum shop that contributes to customer loyalty and customer identification.

Despite all the digitality, "classic" analogue PR work should not be ignored. Especially when a virtual museum goes out into the world with hybrid formats such as time-limited *pop-up museum events*. The virtual world will not replace personal encounters. We will not dissolve into the metaverse; people are not digital beings.

5. ADDED VALUE

5.1 Value proposition and competitive advantages of virtual museums

(JULIA RÖMHILD)

In general, the value proposition of virtual museums can certainly be summed up as follows: *Interconnected knowledge and culture. For everyone. Always. Everywhere.*

A value or benefit proposition also represents the unique selling proposition (USP), i.e. the unique selling point from the perspective of the respective cultural practitioner or cultural organisation that makes a cultural offer (cf. Homburg 2020, p. 621; Günter/Römhild 2023, p. 78). This is an argument as to why the offer is worthy of preference. Only when such a feature of a cultural offering is also perceived as such by the target groups addressed, i.e. the audience, can a competitive advantage be realised over relevant rival offerings. Accordingly, competitive advantages can only be realised if they relate to service components of a provider that are

- are relevant from the target groups' point of view,
- are perceptible to them and which can be
- permanently and efficiently
- defended against the competition (see Meffert et al. 2019, p. 59).

In order to identify unique selling points and thus potential competitive advantages on the part of virtual museums, it is first important to understand the type of museum services – in general and in the special case of virtual museums, as described in chapter three.

The general overall objective of cultural organisations can certainly be defined as making art and culture possible and accessible to the public. The services offered by museums are predominantly cultural services. This raises the following questions:

- What is the nature of services?
- What can be the core and additional services of virtual museums?
- What is the nature of the service in the virtual space as opposed to the analogue museum?
- What are the (potential) competitive advantages for virtual museums?
- What value proposition results from this?

Services are independent, marketable offerings (see Meffert et al. 2019, p. 29) that are associated with the provision and use of capabilities. In the case of virtual museums, these provision services are primarily of a non-physical nature (digital instead of analogue exhibition spaces, online shops, etc.). The process of creating services requires a combination of internal and external factors. The digital spaces, exhibits and information, games and live tours that are made available will only realise their full potential if digital visitors make use of the services, get involved and participate. The challenge here certainly lies in the design of the "encounter" with the visitors and, if necessary – for example through the use of avatars – the visitors among themselves.

In the following, an attempt will be made to identify potential competitive advantages for virtual museums that could possibly be used to position them in a competitive environment. A basic distinction can be made between four types of positioning-relevant competitive advantages:

The *quality or benefit advantage* refers to superior characteristics of the offer and thus superior benefits for the customer compared to competing offers. Quality can refer to the content of the museum: In this way, niche topics that have previously been difficult or impossible to capture in physical form in museums can be covered. From a formal point of view, it is possible to virtually convey other "types of knowledge" (e. g. practical knowledge) via new ways of imparting knowledge (see formats in chapter 13) such as gamification, tutorials etc. in combination with virtual reality applications. Virtuality also allows for completely different exhibition designs and other types of spaces and can thus become a quality advantage through innovative web design. The aspect of (globally) interconnected knowledge can also contribute to the development of a centre of excellence. Another quality aspect could lie in the possibility of participation: co-creation through the use of crowdsourcing and swarm intelligence. "Physical accessibility" can also make virtual museums preferable. However, "virtual accessibility" for blind and deaf people must be considered from the very beginning of the design process. The use of social XR at live events in virtual museums also allows hundreds of visitors to come together at the same time, experience culture together, have fun and get to know each other. Or two friends can meet up for an exhibition opening, even though one lives in Germany and one in the USA. The only thing that needs to be coordinated is the timing, as the visitors may be physically located on different continents. Social contacts and shared experiences can be maintained and shared without much coordination effort and money for travelling.

A *cost advantage* is aimed at an advantage through lower costs on the part of the customer. This refers to the total cost of ownership (adapted here: total cost of visitorship or total cost of participation), i. e. all monetary costs incurred by the visitor – tickets, guided tours, paid content, but also: energy costs when using the virtual museum, costs for hardware acquisition and operation, etc. These are probably – but depending on the revenue model, not necessarily – lower than for a comparable visit to an analogue museum, for which travel costs, parking fees, etc. may also be incurred. In every planning scenario, the willingness of the public to pay for tickets, for example, must be taken into account, which may be lower in the digital space.

The *time advantage* relates to the faster availability of offers and services. Virtual museums are per se available at any time and, in principle, everywhere. They are not tied to opening hours, dates and locations, but time-based virtual events are also conceivable and useful for generating and utilising preferences.

The *reliability advantage* arises when a provider is more likely to fulfil its performance promise than the competition. In the virtual space, reliability can certainly be achieved in particular through sufficiently high server capacities and thus online accessibility. Since reliability is based on trust, a virtual museum must use various mechanisms to build trust with its stakeholders, e.g. through personnel elements of the website, guarantees, honouring promises, etc.

The potential competitive advantages identified must certainly be adapted to the content and structure of the virtual museum in question. They should be focussed accordingly – most likely in the area of quality benefits. In addition, it must be checked whether the claimed competitive advantages are relevant and perceptible from the public's point of view.

In connection with the positioning of the offer, it is important to know what kind of competition virtual museums face. The question that arises here concerns the market definition: How "narrow" or "broad" is competition defined? Are only virtual museums considered competition? Analogue museums? Is the perspective broadened to include all types of cultural offerings? Or virtual offerings? Games?

The answer essentially depends on the definition of the target group (chapter 4). It should at least be questioned whether the digital audience of virtual museums is not also considering analogue competitors.

5.2 How sustainable can virtual museums be from a business ecology perspective? (REBECCA HEINZELMANN AND LAURA ZEBISCH)

The potential to achieve a reduction in greenhouse gas emissions through digitalisation is high (Hessian State Chancellery 2021, p. 42). In recent years, however, it has been accompanied by a steady increase in energy and resource requirements (see WBGU 2019, p. 9). An estimated 1.8 to 3.2 % of global greenhouse gas emissions in 2020 are attributable to the production, use and disposal of digital devices and infrastructures (cf. Brüggemann 2021). Digital technologies have a range of obvious environmental impacts (e.g. energy consumption) and hidden consequences (e.g. material degradation). Their ecological footprint is made up of, among other things, the electricity used to operate the technical devices, the raw materials used in the manufacturing process, the emissions released during data transmission and the work of the data centres.

But how can the ecological footprint of virtual museums be recorded and reduced?

One way to compare physical and virtual museums in terms of their "environmental footprint" is to use the *Green Cloud Computing (GCC)* assessment methodology (see UBA 2021, p. 42–43). This is based on the formula

$$GCC = \frac{Costs}{Benefits}$$

(cf. ibid., p. 52). It can also be used, for example, to calculate the CO2 emissions for the provision of a virtual service, i.e. also a virtual museum visit. A suitable reference value (unit of account) must first be defined, which applies to both the analogue and digital space with all the associated contributing parameters and for which the benefits (section 5.1) and costs can be worked out. It is obvious to use the average length of stay in a museum, which is between one or two hours (cf. Schößler 2020), or the possible sustained attention that can be provided for twenty minutes during the reception of exhibition content (cf. Höge 2016, p. 272), with regard to the museum visit service. This is also interesting considering the different utilisation intensities of different target groups (section 4.1). An explanation of the exact calculation method for determining the GCC key figure(s) would go too far at this point, but can be found in detail and with regard to application in the UBA study mentioned at the beginning (see UBA 2021, pp. 106–137).

Irrespective of the comparison of the environmental compatibility of physical and virtual museums, the following short- to long-term questions and measures should be clarified in advance of the establishment of a digital institution or in the case of a virtual museum that is already in operation. There is no claim to completeness here! The choice of strategy used to address the questions listed below has a strong influence on the derivation of the associated sustainability objectives. In order to contribute to a culture of sustainability in the long term (see Römhild and Heinzelmann 2023 as an example) and to support the socially desired sustainability transformation, the sufficiency strategy should be considered in addition to efficiency and consistency strategy approaches (see Hahn 2022, p. 30–40 for an example of the sustainability strategies). Sufficiency is about acting and consuming less, more slowly and regionally by scrutinising the focus on needs. The aim is to use, reuse, avoid and/or reduce consumption for as long as possible. *User-centred* or *human-centred design* are one possible key to this. This needs to be discussed and scrutinised. In addition to the sufficiency strategy, Santarius and Lange postulate guiding principles for sustainable digitalisation. This also includes digital sufficiency with the creative leeway of *technology sufficiency, data sufficiency* and *usage sufficiency* (Santarius and Lange 2018, p. 143–166). These were also taken into account when formulating the short- to long-term questions and measures.

The following are short and medium-term issues and measures that can be used to meet the challenge of environmentally sustainable digitalisation:

- Which electricity is used or should be used to operate the virtual museums website? Switching to green electricity increases the share of renewable energy in total energy consumption and reduces the consumption of fossil fuels. It should therefore be checked whether the website host uses green electricity. This can be done with various tools (e. g. the Website Carbon Calculator, available online at **https://www.websitecarbon.com**) or with direct enquiries.
- Is the design of the website or the digital route in my virtual museum user-friendly? In other words, can unnecessary clicks be avoided, even if clicks are a success parameter (Chapter 4.2, 15.4)?
- Are the servers and data storage products that are used environmentally friendly and, if necessary, even certified? (further information UBA 2022)

- What are the default settings for the resolution of the digital exhibition objects and images? The lowest possible resolutions are recommended for the mere preview.
- Are automatic playbacks of videos avoided? Around 60–70 % of the global data volume is accounted for by streaming films (cf. Brandt 2020).
- Can the creation of digital duplicates be avoided by using the storage of data on the Europeana or museum-digital servers to integrate the digital collection, for example?
- Cookies: What data do I really need? How much data traffic needs to be generated and stored?

Long-term infrastructural decisions that should either already be integrated into the planning of virtual museums or can be used to reflect on existing structures are, for example:

- How energy-efficient is the technology (hardware) that is used? Is it worth switching to devices certified with the Blue Angel eco-label in the long term?
- How data-intensive does the software that is developed really need to be? It should be desirable for the virtual museum to be technically designed in such a way that it works flawlessly on hardware (laptops, smartphones, etc.) of different ages and that it rarely needs to be replaced (see Santarius and Lange 2018, p. 152). From a technical perspective, it is important to write the museum's code in such a way that it can be easily expanded on a modular basis (keyword: longevity of the virtual museum). Open source and open access should also be considered so that knowledge can be used sustainably and resources are not tied up unnecessarily (see Team Z museum4punkt0 2021). A key question here is: Can the digital infrastructure of the virtual museum be reused or repurposed for other projects?
- Are users and visitors of virtual museums sensitised and trained with regard to responsible digital use? Can the museum provide usage recommendations regarding resolution settings, etc.?
- Are environmental goals and values also taken into account by the AI that may be used in the virtual museum or by its underlying code? How adapted is the AI code to socio-ecological goals? (cf. Gailhofer 2023, p. 3, 13) It is worth mentioning at this point that there is still too little data available on the consequences of AI applications for the climate and environment in terms of energy and resource consumption to be able to make really reliable statements on this (keyword rebound effect), especially once they have become established and their use is commonplace. This also applies to the use of AI specific to the museum, such as when guiding visitors through the virtual museum. Ecological criteria and indicators to be scrutinised can be found in "Sustainability criteria for artificial intelligence – development of a set of criteria and indicators for the sustainability assessment of AI systems along the life cycle" by Algorithm Watch.
- What is digitised and made digitally accessible with the help of a virtual museum should be questioned at regular intervals: How is content perceived? What indicators show the utilisation of exhibits in a virtual museum? What happens if exhibits are

neither clicked on nor consumed after a defined period of time? Are there fixed time periods (similar to exhibition times) after which content changes? Which content is consumed by which target groups? (Keyword: long-term archiving or fluctuating information: Which data should be preserved in exponentially growing mass storage systems?)

In addition to the short-term and long-term questions and measures that need to be addressed in the context of virtual museums, there is also some potential that virtual museums can bring with them in terms of the environmentally friendly and careful use of digital infrastructures and end devices:

- Savings in CO_2 emissions by not transporting exhibits and artworks for special exhibitions.
- Savings in CO_2 emissions by reducing public transport and nevertheless global networking (Chapter 5.1) (see Bitkom 2020, p. 36).
- Reduction of commuting trips through working from home or reduction of business trips through video conferencing (calculation example in UBA 2021, p. 136).
- Resource savings are possible because no material-intensive museum buildings are created, there is no printed supplementary material or resource-intensive exhibition reconstructions and no physical exhibition furniture is required. Nevertheless, the consumption of resources in connection with the hardware and operation of the digital infrastructure should not be underestimated (see Bitkom 2020, p. 11).

A conclusive comparison of the environmental impact of physical and virtual museums is only possible to a very limited extent, as the quality, characteristics and environmental factors of the museums compared would have to be the same. Furthermore, a complete eco-balance cannot be mapped, as comprehensive studies would also have to take into account "the energy consumption of the respective workplaces (e. g. heating energy, lighting), the change in consumer behaviour (e. g. kitchen, canteen, clothing), the rebound effects (e. g. additional meetings, duplicate office equipment) and possibly other factors" (UBA 2021, p. 135). Digitalisation should not be an end in itself. Every digital action, every digital product and every digital service has an environmental impact, just like in the analogue world. It is important to uncover the connections between digitalisation and the environment and to reflect on them using the questions raised in this chapter.

6. BUSINESS MODEL

6.1 The founders journey: From the idea to the business plan (REINHARD GRÖNE)

Anyone involved in setting up a museum – and this also applies to the virtual museum – is embarking on a complex journey. For validation, a four-stage process is recommended, which all types of organisations should go through. This ensures that at the end of the journey, a museum is created that fits into the landscape in a credible, relevant and resilient way and that has a secure footing, i. e. a sufficient budget so that it does not have to close again soon or cannot be opened in the first place. Just like land and building materials, architects and structural engineers, the virtual museum also needs professional foundations and partners: Internet providers, resilient servers, programmers, designers, suppliers of verbal and visual content, possibly some kind of editorial team and curatorship.

What applies to the founding phase continues in later operations: museum management, curation, exhibition content and a constant stream of new impulses and/or attractions that are able to attract visitors worldwide 24/7.

For an initial "quick check", there are six sets of questions:

- Which topic has been identified that is worthy of being honoured and presented in a museum? And what is interesting for visitors, users and experts?
- How are the aspects of "collecting, preserving, researching, exhibiting and communicating" organised?
- What makes the museum unique? How can it become a long-term audience-magnet?
- What is the museum's business model? Does it rely exclusively on public funding? Is a "hybrid" conceivable, e. g. a public-private partnership? Or will it be run entirely by the private sector?
- What skills is/are the founder(s) lacking? What support from experts is needed to avoid failure?
- What will make the museum exciting in ten years' time? How will it present itself? Where is it located in the "metaverse"?

In the second step, a more detailed operator and business model is developed. A business model canvas derived from Osterwalder's original helps with this.

The "BusinessMap", borrowed from the ecosystem "start-up", highlights all the necessary factors that every company should consider if it wants to exist sustainably. It is irrelevant in which order the individual aspects, from market relevance to existing skills, are filled with reliable content. The BusinessMap is a "dashboard" that can be used associatively, a thematically pre-sorted mind map that collects all possible key factors and puts them to the test. A complex process that requires constant reflection as to whether a newly verified aspect has an impact elsewhere or even appears counterproductive.

And if, at the end of the day, profits are not at least in the black, it may be necessary to rethink or, at worst, look for a more pragmatic approach. Without a functioning business model, even the best of ideas will fall by the wayside.

The BusinessMap is a further development of the Business Model Canvas (BMC) by Alexander Osterwalder from "Business Model Generation", Frankfurt 2008.

<table>
<tr>
<td rowspan="2">Market relevance

Problem solving?
Innovation?
Disruption potential?</td>
<td>Service / Transaction object

Offer?
Product?
Service?
Rights?
Patents?</td>
<td colspan="2">Value proposition

Unique position?
Customer need?
Customer benefit?</td>
<td>Communication

Positioning?
Advertising?
PR?
Customer Journey?</td>
<td>Customers, target groups

Core, Mass, Niche segments?
B2C?
B2B?
B2B2C?</td>
</tr>
<tr>
<td>Bottlenecks

Own resources?
External resources?
Market potential?</td>
<td colspan="2">Competitive advantage

Price/Performance?
Quality?
Availability?</td>
<td>Sales & distribution channels

Online? Offline?
Lead & customer acquisition?
Offers?
After sales?</td>
<td>Customer loyalty / Relationship channels

Community?
Network?
Social media?
Appreciation?</td>
</tr>
<tr>
<td colspan="3">Cost structure & cost level

Direct & overhead costs? Fixed & variable costs?
Resources? Partners? Suppliers?
Marketing & sales?</td>
<td>Profit

Turnover
minus
costs</td>
<td colspan="2">Sales / Sources of revenue

Sale? Usage? Membership fees? Leasing?
Licenses? Subscription? Offers?
Sales promotions? Discounts? Auctions?</td>
</tr>
<tr>
<td colspan="6">What drives me? What are my entrepreneurial skills?

Purpose? Mission? Vision? Scalability?</td>
</tr>
</table>

Figure 1: Angel Engine e. V. BusinessMap

The third step involves an understandable, striking self-presentation of the museum idea. This can be a multi-page presentation, comparable to a "pitch deck", as has proven successful in the "start-up" ecosystem. However, it can also be a short explanatory film, which – in keeping with the theme – can contain digital AR and VR elements.

To be addressed:

- Introduction: Mission and purpose of the museum
- About the contents of the collection: What does the museum offer its visitors, also for repeat visits?
- How are the museum requirements met?
- Who and how big are the target groups?

- What do visitors expect from the museum?
- What expertise is behind the founding team?
- How will the museum be financed in the medium and long term?
- How does the museum generate its own income?
- Who are the museum's potential competitors?

The fourth step is to develop a robust business model and a sustainable business plan that convinces all stakeholders and/or partners interested in the museum theme that the virtual museum project makes sense.

Listed below are the key points of a recommendation for the agenda of a "museum plan", which can be structured in a similar way to a classic business plan.

- Management Summary
- Museum and business idea
- Value proposition – benefits – core competences
- Sales – Market & Competition
- Customers – Sales & Communication
- Founders – Team & Partners
- Values – Mission – Purpose
- Company – Legal form & regulations
- Finances: Revenues/sales & costs, capital requirements & financing
- Profitability & liquidity
- Risks

The museum plan should not exceed 30 pages. It should be factual, yet interesting and entertaining. And preferably formulated in the same way. After all, the reader should enjoy the museum idea and find it convincing. In terms of storytelling, it is told in an exciting way with an interesting dramaturgy. This means that right at the beginning of a business and museum plan, it should be made clear which value proposition and thus which benefits are offered to the reader, visitor or other person – first in the planning, then later as a virtual experience in the metaverse.

6.2 The "virtual museum" business model: Building blocks and development
(BERND GÜNTER)

A business model is the concept for the structure and behavioural options of a planned organisational process within the framework of an organisational unit or network. In 2001, Ahlert, Backhaus and Meffert published a proposal on how a business model can be appropriately structured.

A business model – including that of a cultural institution – results from a business idea that has already been honed. The first building block consists of a benefit model. This shows which benefit or value proposition is given to target groups, customers (users, visitors) – in general: stakeholders. A second building block is the so-called revenue model. It should answer the question of how prices/revenues (e. g. admission prices, purchase prices, etc.) are formulated in return for the addressee. Examples of revenue models include Unit prices per visit, subscriptions, ArtCards, etc. A third, comprehensive building block is the "system architecture". This module contains considerations regarding location, organisational structure, offline or online communication and distribution channels, cooperation partners, etc.

A business model understood and structured in this way does not necessarily have to be geared towards making a profit; it can also be applied to cost recovery or other less commercial or even non-commercial structures. A "business plan" is derived from a business model with more specific planning details on the various organisational elements that will define the subsequent operations.

For a virtual museum, value propositions can be thought of that are formally linked to each of the ICOM museum tasks and also to the suitability criteria listed in chapter three. In terms of content, the value model depends on the planned content, on "collection content" and its benefits for different addressees.

If the virtual museum is to be operated economically, consideration must at least be given to generating revenue that goes beyond a lump sum sponsorship to cover costs. Possible options include one-off payments from users, such as when purchasing an app, as well as in-app purchases, but also subscriptions, commissions from content suppliers or revenue from a virtual museum shop. Such offers can be educational programmes, for example.

There are plenty of role models for a business plan from different economic sectors as well as guidelines on the ideal structure of a business plan – including from the Federal Ministry for Economic Affairs and Climate Protection[1] . It is important to always keep the benefits for the target groups and their loyalty at the centre of your considerations.

1 Cf. the BMWK handout: **GründerZeiten Nr. 07: Businessplan** and the BMWK website on business start-ups, URL: **https://www.bmwk.de/Redaktion/DE/Dossier/existenzgruendung.html** [accessed on 13 June 2024].

6.3 The business plan: Digital partly different than analogue

(REINHARD GRÖNE AND BERND GÜNTER)

A business plan serves to substantiate a business model and thus clarify to external stakeholders, but also to the founders themselves, which components need to be planned and implemented in order to get a business "up and running" and manage it in a targeted manner. A business plan should begin with the marketing components of target groups, customer benefits and value proposition and end, for example, with the opportunities and risks of the aspects mentioned in the meantime.

In the case of a virtual museum, the following aspects must be taken into account:

- Digital target groups can behave differently than "analogue" museum users
- The transaction costs for using virtual offers are different and often lower
- The revenue model of the virtual museum poses different and new challenges. There are questions of an access fee, possibly a subscription, external financing, questions of in-app purchases or included advertising or market research that contribute to financing.

In general, the virtual museum can be seen as a two-sided institution (like most media): The system architecture of the virtual museum can or should be open to the participation of many stakeholders, e. g. via user-generated content. The language used is a central problem here – unless non-visual content is thematised without language. The structure of the navigation and underlying hardware and software developments must be taken into account, etc.

HOLGER SIMON

7. TECHNICAL REQUIREMENTS

Virtual museums, collections and exhibitions are digital offerings that visitors can use and visit online.

In contrast to the "analogue museum", visitors always need an interface, i. e. hardware with software specific to the application. (Today, most digital offerings are accessed and launched online via a browser or a local application such as apps. In both cases, data can be exchanged in both directions. However, there are also applications, such as some early VR/AR applications, which have to be installed locally on the desktop PC or VR glasses and then operate completely autonomously. They only draw resources from the Internet when required.

We can differentiate between virtual museums, collections and exhibitions on two levels: a) in the spatial presentation of the objects and b) in the social interaction (social networks) between visitors. Depending on the combination, different types and technical requirements arise.

A. No spatial presentations/no social interaction

Most digital offerings present their collection objects in lists and detailed pages (Europeana, Museum digital, etc.). With its **digital collection** digital collection, the Städel Museum has begun to break up the list presentation and realise specific user experiences (UX) such as digital strolling and random finding as a web application. **Google Arts and Culture** is also experimenting with the possibilities of non-spatial presentations of collection objects.
Technical requirements: Browser

B. 2D applications/no social interaction

Two-dimensional applications are very common as maps and are used in many applications to localise collection objects. In conjunction with GPS, the objects can also be instantly linked to the current location of the visitors, e. g. from the public space.
Technical requirements: Browser, GPS function (smartphone, tablets)

C. 2D applications/social interaction

Applications for social interaction in two-dimensional space were developed for distributed working. Gather.town and SpatialChat became very popular during the coronavirus pandemic. In these two-dimensional spaces, you can move around with an avatar and communicate with others in the room via chat and video. The "owners" of the rooms must register to use the applications, but users can often join the rooms without registering. Although the

rooms of most applications can be customised and exhibition rooms can be started, there are rarely applications from the memory institutions.
Technical requirements: Browser, local applications, login required

D. 3D applications/no social interaction

1. 360 degree panoramas

360-degree panoramas have become established for the presentation of a room (Anne Frank – The Secret Annex). Ten years ago, their production was very complex and expensive, but today they can be produced very easily and inexpensively by museums using commercially available 3D cameras such as Insta360 and presented via the website, for example. Social interaction with others is not possible there. However, they are often used for live online tours and shown via a video conferencing tool.
Technical requirement: Browser

2. Augmented reality

With augmented reality, digital content can be shown in the real world. Visitors need a smartphone or tablet with a camera for this. The specific programme must also be installed on the device. Digital offerings with AR are already available in several museums as additional information in the collection (**Museum Schloss Rheydt**).
Technical requirements: Tablet, smartphone with application

3. Virtual reality

With virtual reality, visitors can immerse themselves audiovisually in a room (immersion). To do this, they need VR glasses with the specific programme. Virtual reality is particularly widespread in games and is expensive to produce.
Technical requirement: VR glasses with application

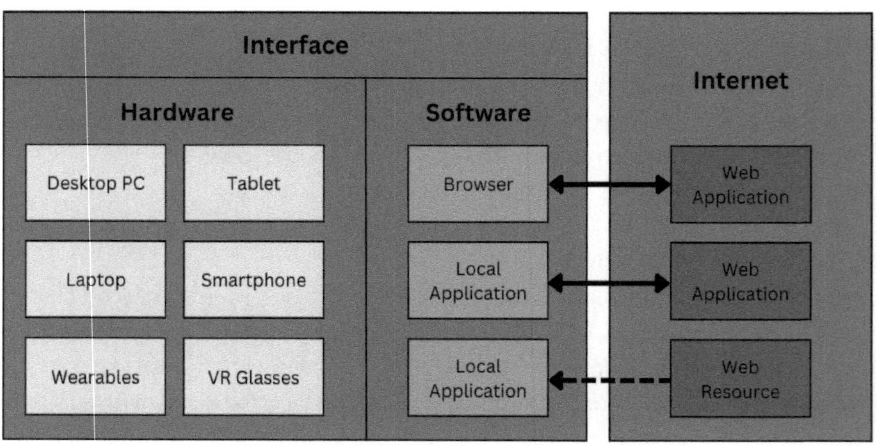

Figure 2: Technical requirements of 3D applications without social interactions

E. 3D applications/social interaction

Welcome to the metaverse. Thanks to high bandwidths and the enormous improvement in video and audio quality in commercially available devices, such as smartphones and webcams, it is now possible for us to have synchronized audio-visual events where we meet and move in digital space. One driver was and is the games industry. For the past three to four years, not only have major players such as Facebook (Group: Meta) and Disney been pushing into this market, but there are also many start-ups with new offerings for virtual immersive applications. The Mozilla Hubs technology offers a very simple way to develop a VR space in which people can then meet as avatars, such as in the spaces of the "area for virtual art" (**https://areaforvirtual.art**). In Spatial.io, museums can create virtual exhibition spaces (**https://spatial.io**). Many billions of dollars have been invested in 3D social networks, such as Decentraland or AltspaceVR, over the past five years or so. These platforms often utilise blockchain technology. DFC Francisco Carolinum took advantage of this and was one of the first art museums to publish a branch in Cryptovoxels with NFT art and still uses this virtual space today. This puts us right in the middle of Web 3.0, in which the distance from real places as the greatest barrier to encounters is removed and proximity is created in a new form of perception.

Technical requirements: Browser, VR glasses, application, login

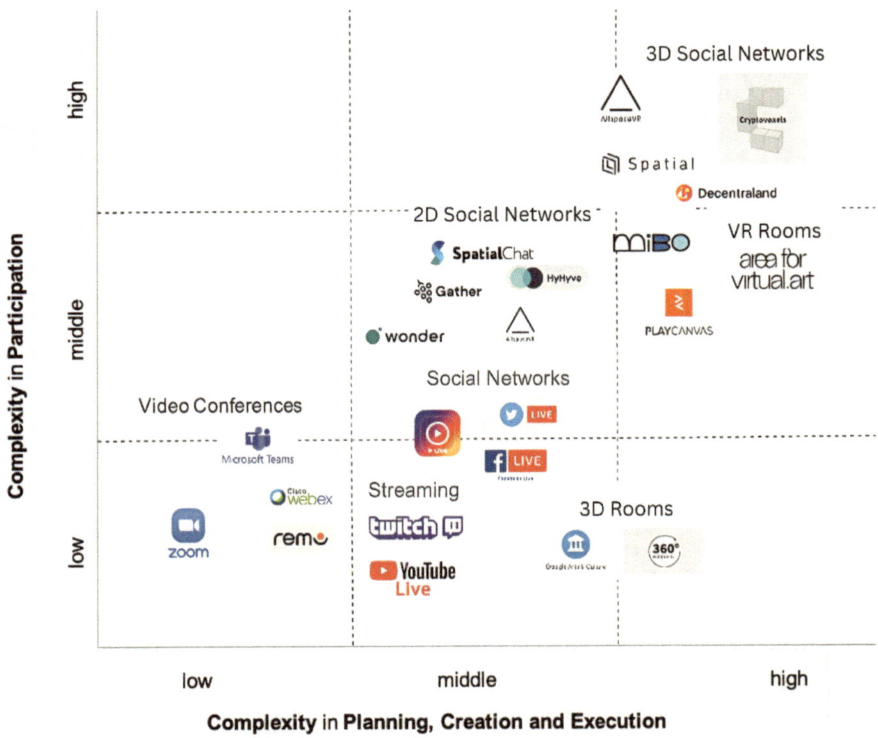

Figure 3: Technical requirements of 3D applications with social interactions

The aspect of user navigation requires special attention when programming a virtual museum. Just as in the analogue case, an external and an internal museum guidance system must be planned and implemented and, above all, adapted to visitor behaviour, software-relevant decisions must also be made for a virtual museum about possible visitor and user guidance and about the shortest and most intuitive steps possible for visitors to move forwards, backwards and disruptively.

ANJA KIRCHER-KANNEMANN

8. RESEARCH

For the time being, it can be said that virtual museums are suitable for increasing the chances of intensive research. This is a consequence of ubiquity, i. e. accessibility anywhere in the world, and access at any time "around the clock" by any researcher, established or "official", in institutions or by individuals, professionally or as a hobby ("amateur").

Research objects in virtual museums as well as information, research theses and results are thus the subject of universal discourse – insofar as the Internet is available and accessible and no censorship or selection takes place.

These statements must be qualified with regard to the language used. However, universal accessibility is facilitated by the use of a "lingua franca", usually English, by the use of mathematical formulae and symbols and by the use of images (photo, video, 2D and 3D) and sound, supplemented by AR and VR applications. There are also opportunities for universal access through the perfection of translation programmes such as DeepL.

In terms of content, the application of these technological possibilities can be particularly interesting for

- Objects (artefacts) that may not be removed from their physical location for conservation and other reasons
- Market research, e. g. surveys on art and culture, where knowledge of the materials presented and rapid evaluation are desirable
- In other use cases as listed in chapter three

The new ICOM definition of museums adopted in Prague in 2022 has placed research at the top of the list of museum tasks and thus created a new focus in the work of museums. The research context will also increasingly give museums the role of "competence centres" in the future – an idea that Prof. Bernd Günter has been advocating for several years (section 2.1.) Since museums have always had the task of being places of education and mediation, it makes sense and is also forward-looking to give research a higher priority and to place it at the centre of museum work, especially since research makes the museum a forum for national and international exchange. This makes museums a central location for researchers, people interested in specific topics and cultural professionals.

Research in museums is traditionally primarily research on objects. The primary aim is to gather information about the object in order to explain and narrate its history and context. Research thus serves both the conception of new exhibitions and the production of new publications and provides the basis for provenance research, which is becoming increasingly important.

Virtual museums can make a special contribution here, as their collections already exist in digital form and can therefore be made available worldwide. This increases the chances of intensive research work. They therefore offer added value to small and medium-sized museums in particular, as they are often unable to digitise their collections due to a lack of human resources.

However, only research enables museums to design exhibitions in a sustainable, future-oriented and scientifically sound manner and thus fulfil their mandate to educate and impart knowledge. This is how research generates knowledge. This knowledge can then be transformed into education through exhibitions, publications, lectures and other events and forms of presentation.

Research at museums can be carried out in co-operation with university and non-university institutions from the fields of culture, science and business, which is already the case in many museums. This also helps museums to step out of their niche or ivory tower and become part of the social discourse.

9. COLLECT

9.1 Collecting in virtual museums
(ANJA KIRCHER-KANNEMANN)

A museum's collection, whether virtual or analogue, is its foundation. The digital recording of the collection holdings is at the centre of the digital strategy. This is particularly true for virtual museums. For them, too, it is necessary to keep an eye on the focal points of their own collection, to check for gaps, to compare their own holdings with those of similar museums and to derive a collection strategy from this. In this way, the museum serves the central task of permanently preserving evidence from the past and present.

The collection is also the basis for other museum tasks, such as research and documentation. Collection work includes the documentation of the collection, inventorying, object-related research work and the integration of new research findings.

In the digital domain, a large proportion of this data is subsumed under the term metadata. Metadata is structured data that contains information about the characteristics of objects. This includes, for example, size, material, provenance, date of origin, details of the manufacturer, literature references, etc.

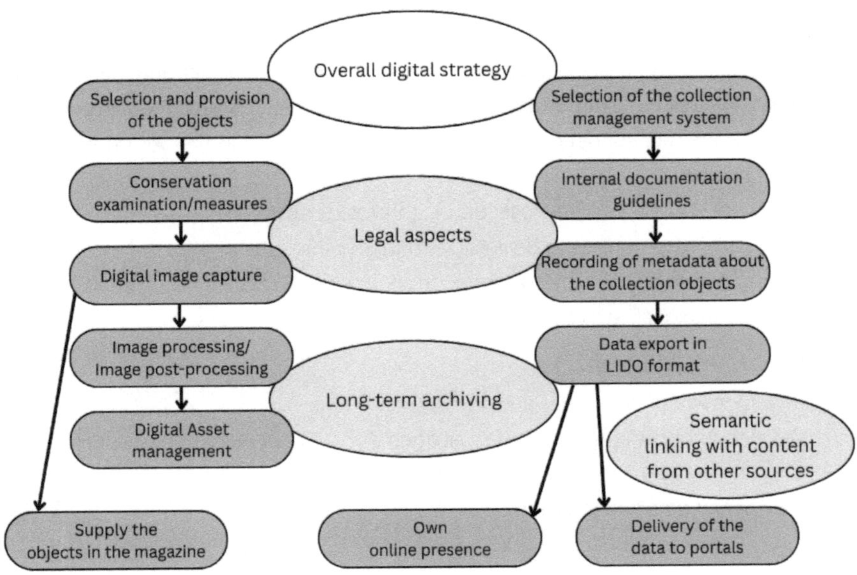

Figure 4: Representation of a typical collection indexing process

When dealing with collections in virtual museums, it must first be clarified whether these are also of a purely virtual nature or whether they are physical or hybrid. Depending on the type of collection, the ways in which the collection is created and expanded, how it is handled and, if applicable, how it is presented will differ. But just as with collections of analogue objects, virtual museums also need a collection profile, as well as a collection strategy, collection maintenance and collection documentation.

Virtual museums can ultimately even become particularly important for research with regard to their collection, as they have completely digitised their objects and provided them with metadata and can therefore make them available ubiquitously, which is not yet the case with analogue stationary museums (cf. Klinke 2023).

9.2 Collection care

(ANJA KIRCHER-KANNEMANN)

In the case of a virtual museum based on a purely virtual collection, collection management is very different from the management of an analogue stationary museum. All areas dedicated to the preservation and storage of analogue artefacts are omitted here. They are replaced by the maintenance and preservation of digital data. However, this is a task that is also increasingly falling to analogue museums, so that ultimately the tasks are similar in this respect too.

A digital collection requires staff who are just as familiar with the digital world as they are with collecting. The combination of both areas leads to a new professional field, that of the digital collection curator. However, current museum training programmes have so far been inadequate, making it difficult to find suitable people for this field – a problem that museums are increasingly facing.

When maintaining a digital collection, the contextualisation and networking of the existing data is particularly important. There is no one-size-fits-all solution. Collection maintenance and management depend on the financial basis as well as the personnel and the respective concept.

The central task of a digital collection is to provide structured data (metadata) that allows data from other sources to be linked and thus enables the objects to be contextualised. Only in this way is it possible to further develop the collection.

Basic tasks in digital collection maintenance:

- Digital recording of objects
- Development of descriptive and administrative data
- Development of digital collection management
- Ongoing maintenance of the data and the system
- Provision of data for exhibitions.

9.3 Further development of the collection

(ANJA KIRCHER-KANNEMANN)

The basis for the further development and expansion of a virtual museum collection is – just as in the analogue field – good and constant research into the central themes of the museum. A functioning network is helpful in order to obtain and integrate new digital or physical collection items. The clarification of usage rights is probably even more important for virtual museums than for analogue museums. They are therefore discussed in detail in Chapter 16.

The establishment and further development of a digital collection also means always keeping an eye on new developments. This applies to developments in the area of presentation as well as those in the areas of education, contextualisation and, above all, technology. The following points need to be taken into account during further development:

- Relevance of the objects for research
- Interest of the public in the object
- Accessibility of the object
- Legal aspects (copyright/licences), see chapter 16
- Available information
- Link to the previous collection
- Closing gaps
- Opportunities for co-operation with other institutions
- Financing etc.

The aim should be to turn the collection into a knowledge database that enables users to obtain comprehensive information about the museum and its collection and to enable stakeholders to participate digitally.

9.4 Archiving

(ANJA KIRCHER-KANNEMANN)

Archiving is based on compliance with international standards. It ensures the sustainability of the digitised material provided, not only for the museum's own exhibitions, but also for research purposes. In a virtual museum in particular, archiving is dependent on the digital strategy and serves to build a profile. In addition, it is particularly subjected to technical innovations and therefore dynamic developments.

In addition to human resources and expertise, suitable hardware, software and sufficient storage space must be available for archiving.

Sub-areas of archiving:

- Digital image capture using a scanner or digital photography
- 3D reconstructions, laser scanning, etc. This may require external service providers

- Image processing (RAW, TIFF, WebP) – current minimum standard is TIFF format, 24-bit colour depth for RGB and a minimum resolution of 300 dpi
- Digital asset management: organisation, indexing, provision of digital files, see: **https://collectionstrust.org.uk/spectrum/**
- Metadata: Date of recording, other recording data such as the name of the photographer(s), camera settings and usage rights, image content, ownership information, legal information, location of the object, information on the object's history, contextualisation, references in literature, information on the artist, etc., see: **https://cidoc.mini.icom.museum/working-groups/documentation-standards/**, **https://www.dnb.de/DE/Professionell/Standardisierung/GND/gnd_node.html**, **https://test.iconclass.org/**
- Selection of a collection management system
- Data and digital literacy.

To ensure the long-term archiving of digital content, it is necessary to regularly check the hardware, especially the storage media, and replace it if necessary. Regular updates must also be scheduled for operating systems and software programmes. In addition, the archived data must be updated periodically. This also includes adapting the file formats, as is currently the case with the switch from TIFF to WebP.

9.5 Collection operators and collection cooperation

(REINHARD GRÖNE)

- The collection manager has the task of being informed above all about the digital exploitation and usage rights available on the market. Building and expanding the collection requires a direction, the "direction of impact" and, if necessary, thematic or format-related selection mechanisms and prioritisation.
- Collection collaborations can look very different in the digital world than in the analogue world. After all, no exhibits or knowledge documents have to be physically "handed over". It's all about digital usage rights that are shared. Referring back to the original source is a win-win situation for everyone involved. And they can be stored in the blockchain if required.

Collection co-operations – Four examples around *champagne*:

- Specialist publishers and editorial offices around the world already have digitised information about champagne and its production.
- UNESCO has declared champagne and its production a World Heritage Site. Extensive research has been carried out and many sources of information identified.
- The "Comité Interprofessionnel du Vin de Champagne" is a semi-governmental association of independent Champagne producers. The association has probably the most comprehensive digitised archive.

- There is an internet platform that organises digital and analogue exchange markets for "muselets".

Relevant painting and art databases can be used to bring together, curate and exhibit virtual temporary exhibitions that have champagne as their theme.

ANJA KIRCHER-KANNEMANN

10. PRESERVE

The task of preserving cultural assets in a virtual museum is initially similar to that of analogue museums, especially with regard to the objective of conservation. Changes or additions arise primarily in the case of digital products and the digital storage of all objects or all material (section 9.4).

The past has shown that storage media in particular, and thus the activities of storage and transfer, are subject to technical and organisational changes without any certainty of downward compatibility, but with the probability of obsolescence – sooner or later. So it sounds almost banal to always store data in the latest usable and possibly most future-relevant form.

Finally – also due to possible technical changes – the organisation of access and networking via data standards (see the current status of the NFDI discussion), indexing, etc. must be ensured. The necessary access organisation and compatibility also ensure use in the sense of the museum's tasks of researching, collecting, communicating and exhibiting.

11. EXHIBIT AND PRESENT

11.1 Exhibiting and presenting in virtual museums
(ANJA KIRCHER-KANNEMANN)

> A digital exhibition is based on a clear concept and is curated. It assembles, links and disseminates digital multimedia objects to deliver innovative presentations of a theme or series of themes that enable a high degree of interaction with the user (Carius/Fackler 2022).

The digital or virtual space offers numerous possibilities for presentation that are not available in analogue space. This allows exhibitions to be created that were previously not possible in the analogue space. For example, objects can be combined with each other that could not be combined in an analogue museum. AI also has a special role to play in the virtual museum, as it now makes it possible to create objects, such as image documents, that do not actually exist or no longer exist. This enables a completely new and more comprehensive type of contextualisation, which is particularly important for digital objects.

However, most museums that operate under the label "virtual" today do not even come close to utilising these possibilities, but instead present themselves in a form that can hardly be distinguished from a normal website. Exhibitions in the digital space are currently based primarily on parallaxes that allow visitors to scroll through the history or theme. You can integrate video and audio files, as well as extensive image galleries or even 3D applications. In this way, exhibition topics can be communicated using multimedia and difficult topics in particular can be conveyed in a more differentiated way.

VR applications have hardly been used to date. One of the main reasons for this is probably the considerable cost. However, it is precisely the use of this technology that would be a major advantage of a virtual museum, as it could make the thematic world of the museum or the various exhibitions visible and tangible for everyone at any time and in any place. The creation of a (virtual) spatial experience, as is typical for analogue museums, is also little used. What is needed is at least virtual architecture and scenography.

By using these technologies, it would be possible to create additional educational, interaction and participation offerings that exceed the possibilities of the analogue museum to some extent, as there are far fewer virtual boundaries than analogue ones and new exhibition worlds can be created in this way.

11.2 Topics

(ANJA KIRCHER-KANNEMANN)

Especially today, museums are primarily extracurricular places of learning and adult education. They fulfil a social educational mission and therefore have the task of presenting topics in a way that is as generally understandable and appealing as possible. Both the topics and the type of presentation should be orientated towards the target groups.

The selection and treatment of possible topics for a virtual museum depend largely on the question of how the museum wants to deal with its visitors, how much it wants to involve them in its presentation and to what extent it makes subsequent use possible. An initial approach can be made by answering the question for which topics there are no (comprehensive) analogue museums to date.

With the help of digital technologies, a virtual museum can also convey topics that are difficult to present in analogue space. This applies in particular to abstract topics such as "time" or extremely complex topics such as the depiction of an entire epoch. Digitally, it is also possible to tell problematic and complex object stories in an exciting, entertaining and, above all, multimedia-based way. In this way, they become "talking" objects that invite people to engage and reflect, and the virtual museum and its exhibitions are then no longer just "a collection of digital objects", but "an experience, an interactive and immersive platform that allows people to explore and engage with our collections online" (Klinke 2023).

11.3 Curation

(ANJA KIRCHER-KANNEMANN)

Curating is first and foremost the task of selecting objects or texts in order to present them in one place, to transfer them into a structured connection (contextualisation) and to make them speak with the help of storytelling methods in order to introduce and present a topic to an audience. In this respect, curating a virtual exhibition is no different from curating an analogue exhibition. Only the means and the objects available are different and possibly more diverse. So-called complementary exhibitions are also conceivable for virtual museums – especially if they are supplemented by pop-up museums. However, in the case of virtual museums, it is not the virtual but the physical exhibition that is the complement.

In the digital – and ultimately also in the analogue museum space – it is important to know the wishes and needs of the target groups, to take an interest in them and to respond to them in order to be able to run a successful museum.

Digitisation is giving the public a new and more active role. This is particularly true for virtual museums. Participation, involvement and collaboration lead to new models of action and transfer of knowledge. As a result, virtual museums in particular have the opportunity to be perceived as especially approachable, open and communicative, as their digital offerings represent the basic values of digital culture such as openness, mobility, flexibility and user-orientation in a special way.

In the case of virtual museums, curating does not have to be the task of a specialised professional. There are many ways in which co-curation or swarm curation is possible, e.g. with artists or with users/visitors (see the ARTchat approach in the context of Nextmuseum.io) and, in general, the open source idea and considerations regarding user-generated content. The inclusion of AI is just as conceivable.

The paths to the virtual museum taken by visitors represent a challenge in terms of curation, as they are much more varied than in the analogue world. When you enter a museum building, the paths you take are often predetermined, which is due to the sequence of rooms alone. In virtual museums, however, this is not necessarily the case. This offers users the advantage of being able to experience a very individual and unique story, but for curators it means the challenge of thinking through all these possible paths in advance, planning them and checking their consistency – or offering users incentives for a very specific and intentional navigation and thus visitor journey. Ultimately, for curators, this means that each story must be self-contained and make sense, as it is always possible that users will cancel or interrupt their visit in between, go back in the navigation and thus take a different path than the one actually planned. These possibilities must always be taken into account, especially when creating links. In a virtual museum or virtual exhibition, there are no straightforward paths. Visitors can, for example, open an accordion-element, but it is also possible that they will not do so, so they may not be able to "get past" certain information and objects. Such features should therefore only contain information that is actually only additional information, but not necessary for understanding the actual story.

11.4 Exhibition management

(OTMAR BÖHMER)

Exhibitions in analogue or virtual space basically have the same prerequisites and are based on the path from the idea, via research, an initial concept, to checking the available content, via the technical issues to the rights issues and then to implementation and publication. The basis for this can be your own collection; however, co-operation is always an advantage.

These co-operations can be in the fields of content – external collections and works, in the technical possibilities of third parties as well as in the fields of mediation and communication.

This already identifies the areas of work required to realise a virtual project. They are largely identical; some are structured differently and some areas of analogue museum management are not required.

12. COMMUNICATE

12.1 Importance of cultural communication in virtual space
(THERESA STÄRK)

The new version of the ICOM definition of museums adopted in Prague in 2022 changed not only the function but also the tasks of museum institutions. While "to communicate" was previously an integral part of the ICOM definition of a museum, the verb was replaced by "to interpret" in the new version.

ICOM 2007	**ICOM 2022**
"A museum is a non-profit, permanent institution in the service of society and its develop-ment, open to the public, which acquires, conserves, researches, **communicates** and exhibits the tangible and intangible heritage of humanity and its environment for the purposes of education, study and enjoyment."	"A museum is a not-for-profit, permanent institution in the service of society that re-searches, collects, conserves, **interprets** and exhibits tangible and intangible heritage. Open to the public, accessible and inclusive, museums foster diversity and sustainability. They operate and communicate ethically, professionally and with the participation of communities, offering varied experiences for education, enjoyment, reflection and knowledge sharing."

Table 1: Comparison of the ICOM definitions

While the task of "communicating knowledge" focuses much more on visitors or users, the task of "interpretation" emphasises the interpretive sovereignty of museums, whose research and interpretation of the museum object leads to the interpretation that is ultimately presented to the public.

In the new definition, the communication aspect is thematised much more in the second part: *public accessibility*, *accessibility* and *inclusivity* must be part of contemporary education practice. The facilitation of diverse experiences "in terms of education, enjoyment, reflection and knowledge exchange" are central tasks of museum mediation and museum education. According to the new definition of a museum, it is still both a function and a duty of a museum to provide its audience with not only physical, but also emotional and epistemic access to its objects and values. Contemporary, inclusive education forms the starting point for a diverse experience in the museum space.

Accordingly, the chapter is dedicated to "communication", which is no longer mentioned literally in the current museum definition according to ICOM 2022, but can be summarised as such by the points mentioned.

In order to enable low-threshold accessibility to art and cultural objects, not only a digital presentation (independent of location and time) is required, but also a communication that, in addition to the purely aesthetic experience of the objects in virtual space, also transfers knowledge in an audience-orientated way or puts it up for discussion. In addition to the mere visualisation of the objects and publication of the digital copies, accompanying communication is essential for the presentation: according to the previous ICOM definition of the core tasks of a museum (collecting, preserving, exhibiting, researching, mediating), communication is one of the tasks of a museum, including a virtual museum. Diverse communication can reach different target groups and thus create access to cultural assets. According to Carmen Mörsch, in the practice of cultural communication, pedagogical dimensions are interwoven with artistic and social dimensions, ultimately with the aim of realising educational objectives (cf. Mörsch 2012, p. 14). These educational goals can be achieved not only in analogue but also in digital space. While the museum object itself was still the focus of art and museum education in the 1990s, more audience- and action-oriented approaches to educational practice can currently be recognised (cf. Preuß/Hofmann 2017, pp. 13–14). The guidelines for education and outreach published in 2020 by the German Museums Association and the Federal Association for Museum Education advocate education and outreach work that focuses on the individual and society as the core task of a museum. In this context, communication focuses on the museum's perspective and can promote learning processes, including informal ones, among the public. These can be measured according to five success factors: 1. audience-orientation, 2. object-relatedness, 3. diversity of methods and formats, 4. networking, 5. processualism (see Nagel 2020, p. 4–13).

The didactic and creative possibilities of cultural communication in digital space are as heterogeneous as the exhibits themselves. In a virtual museum, there are various ways of communicating digitally displayed objects:

- Analogue existing objects (material/tangible or immaterial/intangible)
- Originally digital objects (*born-digital objects*)
- Intangible objects (intangible).

Each type of object brings its own challenges in digital presentation. Material analogue objects must be digitally reproduced in order to be exhibited in virtual space. The individual digital copies can be visualised in different ways: Two-dimensional or three-dimensional realised as a photo, 3D model with 360° view or as a video.

The absence of the physical (original) object poses new challenges for the communication of art and culture in the digital space: The materially present object can no longer serve as the starting point for personal or media communication, nor can the exhibition space as a situational place of experience and the personal conversation with an educating person or group. Rather, the digitalisation, i. e. the digitally reproduced or originally digital object, is now at the centre of the communication of artefacts in a virtual museum and is dependent on the conditions of the respective web-based platform. At the same time, a virtual presentation offers opportunities for communication: a digital representation can reveal perspectives of an object that may remain hidden in the analogue original – such as the underside of a sculpture, which can be made accessible through a 360° view.

12.2 Implementation possibilities for cultural communication in the digital space

(THERESA STÄRK)

Communication dimensions of knowledge sharing in the analogue exhibition space are classically divided into *medial* and *personal* communication. While in the case of personal communication, a cultural mediator acts as an interface between the work and the viewer as part of a guided tour or a talk in person, media communication is based on impersonal methods such as text-based mediation or digital mediation in the exhibition space, for example through touchscreens, videos, AR, VR, apps, chatbots or audio guides.

In the case of communication through a virtual museum, the possible dimensions of cultural communication are automatically shifted to the digital space, which – apart from the conceivable personalised appearance on the web – means a completely medialised transfer of communication. These can be realised in just as many ways as communication possibilities in the physical exhibition space and are subject in their implementation variations to the ever-advancing technical possibilities of digital transformation.

The cultural communication of a virtual museum can take place in various digital spaces:

1. App-based applications
2. Website
3. Blog
4. Outsourced via software

The fact that a virtual museum is generally web-based means that the integration of an educational tool into the website itself is an obvious choice.

Tools and methods of possible digital cultural communication and thus web-integrated communication in a virtual museum can be categorised according to their degree of interaction, whereby the degree of user-active involvement increases with each further level. Different degrees of interaction:

- *Level 0:* Presentation of the objects through photos with image details without art communication
- *Level 1:* User-passive illustrative and text-based communication methods (educational texts and images)
- *Level 2:* User-passive multimedia communication methods (video/audio formats)
- *Level 3:* User-active multimedia communication methods (gamification elements)

Possible formats that can be categorised into the different levels are

- *Level 0:* Exhibitions with and without accompanying information, individual exhibits, possibly changing regularly
- *Level 1:* Texts, photos of other views of the object and/or to contextualise the work
- *Level 2:* Videos, video tutorials, podcasts, audio files, radio plays
- *Level 3:* Calls for user contributions, games, quizzes, forums, competitions, AR, VR

The higher the level, the greater not only the degree of interaction, but also the degree of audience-orientated participation. "Audience-orientation is a key success factor for effective education and outreach work in museums" (Nagel 2020, p. 18), according to the Guidelines for Education and Outreach published by the German Museums Association and the Federal Association for Museum Education. This applies to analogue as well as digital and hybrid spaces. Through user-active formats such as those of communication level three, users can interact with the virtual exhibition presented through ludic approaches as well as communication and network-based applications, which strengthens the idea of an audience-centred participatory museum.

13. FORMATS

13.1 Definition of "formats"

(BERND GÜNTER)

When the museum tasks of exhibiting (presenting) and communicating are dealt with, the forms of design as the basis of both tasks must be briefly addressed and their diversity highlighted.

"Formats" are forms of design and therefore a kind of framework around content. They can be unidirectional or interactive through to user-generated content. They can be a debt to bring or a debt to collect. They can be visual or acoustic. They can have different people in charge. They can be temporary or permanent, etc.

13.2 Formats of museum presentation and communication

(BERND GÜNTER)

Exemplary formats that can have their place in a virtual museum:

- Exhibitions with and without accompanying information
- Individual exhibits. May change regularly
- Calls for user contributions and their compilation
- Articles and essays
- Lists of exhibition objects with locations
- Photos and photo series
- Films (adopted or specially developed for a virtual museum)
- Webinars
- News and newsletter
- Discussion forums
- Podcasts
- Link and source collections
- Competitions
- Content behind paywalls
- Tips and "recipes", e. g. via **www.calaios.eu**
- 3D models, e. g. modelled via Sketchfab
- Augmented reality applications and experiences
- Virtual reality experiences
- Various open source areas (name them!)
- Gamification elements
- Games, possibly of a simpler nature

- Reviews
- Rating platforms
- Webcams
- Virtual museum architecture
- Community Building
- Shop system
- Localisation in the metaverse (Web 3.0)
- Content depending on the time of day
- Live content
- Curated and public award ceremonies
- etc.

13.3 Excursus: Virtual reality as a format in virtual museums (ISABELLE BECKER)

Virtual museums enable their visitors to view exhibitions and/or collection presentations through various technical implementations in digital space, to examine them more closely and to interact with the individual exhibits. Section 13.2. presented numerous formats in which virtual museum activities can be implemented, whereby the experience for users is in most cases limited to the two-dimensional experience space. In the following, a (communication) format is discussed with which a particularly high degree of user activation and participation can be achieved in the field of art and knowledge transfer: Virtual Reality (VR).

The digital transformation is already permeating all areas of our social and economic activities in a cross-sectional manner and the buzzword "digitalisation" is on everyone's lips, not just in museum circles (see Günter, 2019, p. 220; Hahn, 2021, p. 45). As one of the key technologies of digitalisation, including augmented reality (AR), robotics and artificial intelligence (AI), VR technology is predicted to see high growth and sales increases in the coming years (see Statista, 2022). VR is also becoming increasingly relevant in the art and culture sector; there are already numerous projects that use VR applications as a communication format in the exhibition space[1] .

The users of a VR application find themselves in a (preferably) completely closed, virtual and computer-generated reality – a virtual reality in which they can interact to various degrees. Complete immersion to the point of losing the perception of reality is referred to as *immersion*. Users usually gain access to virtual reality via *head-mounted displays* (HMD), output devices worn on the head such as VR goggles, or by entering projection rooms with

1 Among other things, VR is also part of the federally funded collaboration project museum4punkt0, in the context of which numerous VR projects are/have been realised by various museums throughout Germany (see **https://www.museum4punkt0.de**). The author would like to highlight the so-called "VRlab" of the Deutsches Museum in Munich as an example: the use of VR as a versatile educational tool was researched and documented in detail on a VR experimental area.

large screens, so-called *Cave Automatic Virtual Environments* (CAVE). One example of this, which has been in place since July 2022, is the multimedia installation on the Battle of the Guldensporen in 1302 in the Onze-Lieve-Vrouw church in Kortrijk, Belgium.

The high level of interaction is a unique feature of VR applications. When moving around in a two-dimensional experience space, for example in the form of a 360° panorama, visitors can usually navigate forwards and backwards in more advanced applications and click on individual objects or action fields to obtain the corresponding information (in the form of text, video or audio files). Although the integration of photos enables a realistic representation of the exhibition space, the images become blurred if the user moves very close to the boundaries of the image area. In addition, they can usually only be viewed from one angle and cannot be manipulated by visitors – which makes free exploration and interaction more difficult.

VR enables free navigation and exploration within a virtual environment – depending on the type of application. With the appropriate equipment and depending on the degree of immersion of the application, the elements of the (virtual) exhibition world can be viewed from any desired angle and it is even possible to interact with the exhibits. The selection of individual objects or specific action points in the virtual space is made possible, for example, by means of eye movement control (*eye tracking*) and/or the use of controllers with tracking systems. Compared to static navigation through a two-dimensional exhibition space, navigating with modern VR glasses feels more natural and movements can be transmitted in real time (depending on the model). In addition to intuitive control, VR offers further advantages for virtual museums (see Zouboula et al., 2008, pp. 95–96; Günter, 2019, p. 226; Geipel/Hohmann, 2021, p. 258):

- Environment: By wearing VR glasses with corresponding VR applications, a realistic simulation of the environment and the exhibits is created, intensifying the experience and immersion effect for visitors
- Distance: The actual (physical) distance to the corresponding exhibits can be better suppressed and visitors can immerse themselves in the virtual museum environment independently of time and space and use it (inter)actively.
- Perspective: In VR applications, users can adopt different perspectives. In addition to the first-person perspective, an external perspective or bird's eye view can be adopted, for example
- Immersion: The high degree of immersion makes the virtual world feel real to the user. The phenomenon of fear of heights can also become effective.
- Accessibility (both spatially and thematically): With VR, virtual exhibition worlds can also be visited by people for whom a physical visit is out of the question. In addition, intangible topics can be addressed and particularly fragile objects can at least be experienced virtually.

In an analogue exhibition, effects can be achieved primarily in the area of a realistic recontextualization of certain exhibits, which can already be partially achieved in the virtual museum through the design of the virtual exhibition space and other digital mediation formats. However, the high degree of immersion of a VR application further enhances this effect: original contexts of museum objects can not only be reconstructed in virtual space, but can also be realistically experienced, creating new approaches to the exhibits (cf. Geipel/Hohmann, 2021, p. 258). Initial studies also show that the use of VR in the exhibition context has a positive effect on learning in the museum (see Zouboula et al., 2008, p. 95) and can appeal more strongly to visitors' emotions than other educational tools (see Deutsches Auswandererhaus, 2019, p. 100).

However, the use of VR also harbours challenges and should always be carefully considered and designed for long-term and sustainable use. Firstly, the development, use and (ongoing) maintenance of VR applications are resource-intensive – in terms of time, personnel and, above all, finances. Furthermore, as a relatively new technology, VR is met with scepticism and/or rejection by some visitors. It can also lead to physical reactions in the form of dizziness or nausea (*motion sickness*). In addition, VR applications can be prone to malfunctions and should never be made available without instructions on how to use them and (especially in the case of a virtual museum that can be used independently) contact persons (cf. Geipel/Hohmann, 2021, p. 258). Finally, it must be mentioned that VR must be thought of as an "extension of the [virtual, editor's note] museum space" (Geipel/Hohmann, 2021, p. 258), and by no means as a short-term technical gimmick for the sake of new technology.

Virtual museums harbour the opportunity to transform from occasional and static information tools into means of daily, dynamic, direct and personal contact for visitors, as they can ideally be visited at any time and from anywhere. The simultaneous spread of VR glasses as a hardware solution for the use of VR applications can be a constructive support for the use of virtual content. As VR content becomes more widespread and equipment becomes cheaper to buy (see PWC, 2019), VR applications are a promising communication tool that can boost the development of virtual museums. The potential of VR as a source of income for (virtual) museums should only be briefly mentioned here, in which VR applications can be licensed and sold B2B as templates to other cultural institutions and B2C to end users. Further revenue models for virtual museums are presented in chapter 15.3.

14. ONGOING OPERATION

14.1 Organisational and operational structure
(OTMAR BÖHMER)

In view of the diverse administrative possibilities and the great variety of organisational forms in analogue museums, the "ideal organisational structure" should also be the focus for the virtual museum when deciding on one form or another. It defines the framework of the organisation and provides hierarchical structures according to which the work processes are aligned. All departments, work areas and committees of the institution are organised into a clear structure. The individual sub-units are assigned their tasks and competences, thus ensuring coordination between the sub-units.

The organisational structure therefore defines the framework for which tasks are to be performed by which employees with which resources. The purpose of the organisational structure is to achieve a sensible division of labour and organisation of operational processes by creating and distributing tasks. In concrete terms, this is defined here: Who is in charge? Who decides what? Who is sensibly assigned to whom? What rights and obligations exist for the individual?

The process organisation refers to the completion of tasks – actually the "production process". Everyday work, even in a virtual cultural organisation, is characterised by many processes that have to interlock. Space, places, time and resources are interlinked and should enable the desired goal to be achieved with as little conflict as possible. In order to efficiently and effectively organise the multitude of work processes that take place one after the other and side by side, it is necessary to develop a process organisation that is adapted to the specific requirements.

This concerns details such as the chronological sequence of work steps or the spatial organisation of work processes. The process organisation therefore answers the question: "How, when, where and with what is a subtask performed?" The aim of process organisation is, on the one hand, to optimally utilise the available capacities and, on the other hand, to optimally organise the work process.

With digital collaboration, it can be assumed that work processes can increasingly be carried out in parallel, side by side and more cooperatively. Organisationally, it is less the hierarchy and more the network that is decisive.

The processes will be more time and resource efficient to implement. Appropriate process-orientated software systems must be available for this (e. g. Trello, Slack, MS Project). IT is becoming increasingly important in the "museum" organisation, more so than is already the case today, where digital mediation formats have clearly revealed a lack of expertise in cultural institutions over the last two years. The virtual museum "lives" from the digital holistic approach.

14.2 Alternative forms of self-organisation
(JULIA RÖMHILD)

In order to meet the requirements of digital cooperation, alternative organisational structures can also be considered. In addition to the transfer of "traditional", more hierarchical organisational structures to virtual museums, structures that are usually used in the FinTech and start-up scene are also conceivable. These are "agile" forms of organisation that largely dispense with hierarchical job structures in favour of self-organisation and process orientation.

At the core of agile organisational design is a high level of organisational change dynamics in response to dynamic and often disruptive changes in environmental conditions. The so-called "VUCA world" describes these challenges that cultural organisations have to face (see Mohr/Modarressi 2021). The acronym stands for

- *Volatility* = enormous fluctuations within short periods of time
- *Uncertainty* = difficulty in making clear forecasts
- *Complexity* = increasing density of information to be processed
- *Ambiguity* = contradiction of possible action contexts

In summary, cultural institutions are facing an increasingly ambiguous society, which makes other forms of processing necessary in the sense of a changed way of dealing with everyday issues (cf. Mohr/Modarressi 2021, p. 12) This also requires alternatives to the traditional structural organisation in museums. The following are examples of alternative (or supplementary) concepts that can also be applied to virtual museums in particular:

- *Agility* generally describes the ability to adapt to social changes and can only be achieved through structural elements that promote innovation. In the context of innovation orientation, the keyword *organisational ambidexterity* also appears to be important. Organisational ambidexterity refers to the fact that organisational structures are suitable for making existing processes as efficient as possible (exploitation, for example in relation to administrative tasks), but at the same time also create space for innovation and creativity (exploration). The greater focus on innovation should fertilise or professionalise existing routines through process logic.
- *Collaborative work contexts* follow this logic and can be created as a cross-sectional addition to the organisational structure – usually in the form of projects. The idea is to create a cross-departmental and cross-hierarchical "space" for ideas and self-reflection in order to bring the knowledge of employees into a different relationship with each other and thus enable alternative approaches. (cf. Mohr/Modarressi 2021, p. 19)
- *Agile project management means* that an experienced team with members from different departments takes over the planning and implementation of a project. The team has all the necessary skills and decision-making freedom, always communicates the

progress of the project transparently and continuously coordinates with each other and with other departments. (**https://musermeku.org/agiles-projektmanagement/**)

- *Design thinking* is an agile project management method that is also suitable for cultural organisations (see Pöllmann 2019, p. 91). Essentially, design thinking is an approach from innovation management that combines a variety of questions and methods. The idea of design thinking is to create product or process innovations based on customer needs.
- *Scrum* is another method of agile project management and was first presented to the public at a conference by Jeff Sutherland and Ken Schwaber (1995). The Scrum method contributes significantly to today's understanding of agile working. Scrum uses self-organised teams and shortened planning cycles combined with frequent but also shortened coordination processes.
- *Holacracy* is a form of organisation that is based entirely on self-organisation. Hierarchy and titles are dispensed with; instead, roles are defined that have decision-making autonomy. The organisational structure is divided into "circles" within which roles are defined. The definition of roles is based on the skills that employees bring to the table and distances itself from typical job descriptions. Holacracy follows the view of organisations as organisms that can grow and change and react holistically to challenges. (cf. Deeken/Fuchs 2018, p. 29–31)

The core elements of such structural solutions at project or organisational level are "innovation-promoting structural elements" through dynamization, process orientation, decentralised decision-making structures and the creation of collaborative working contexts. By dispensing with management positions, the decision-making autonomy lies with the employees in the respective specialist or functional areas ("products" or "circles"). However, this also involves frequent and regular coordination processes between all participants.

Agile structural solutions are sometimes well suited or even better for virtual museums that not only primarily address the public digitally, but are also largely organised digitally or based on technology. For example, virtual museums can also be organised virtually and have virtual structures that are largely based on home office and cloud-based coordination and work processes (e. g. using collaborative tools such as Miro, Trello, etc.).

Nevertheless, it must be pointed out at this point that agile structural solutions do not represent a "silver bullet" for organising virtual museums. Rather, it is important to consider whether and to what extent forms of self-organisation can be used, as these require a certain organisational culture with

- a high willingness for cooperative behaviour
- trust
- an open culture of conflict
- an opportunity to exercise authority via professional expertise (not via hierarchical positions)
- the opportunity to act independently (cf. Schreyögg/Koch 2020, p. 357).

It is therefore not (always) possible without "traditional" structures and division of labour. However, agile and innovation-promoting structures can be created to enrich them. Although these must be highly customised and can hardly follow a "recipe". This also applies to the structural organisation of a museum in the classic sense, but this is presented below as an example in order to create a starting point for the structuring of virtual museums that can be changed and expanded as required.

15. SELECTED MANAGEMENT TASKS

15.1 Management and leadership
(OTMAR BÖHMER)

As an example, the (possibly no longer current) organisation chart of the Kunstsammlung Nordrhein-Westfalen is used here as a basis for comparison (see following illustration).

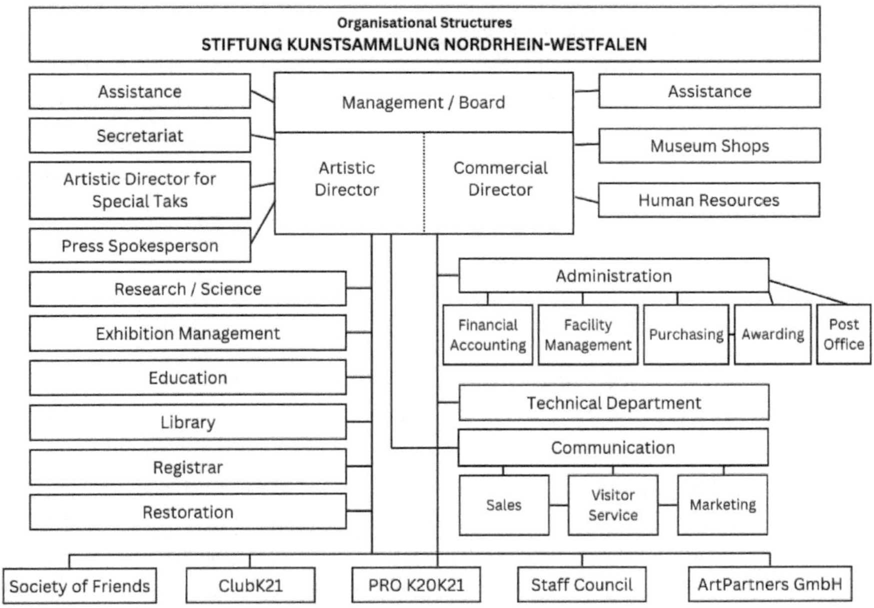

Figure 5: Organisational chart of the Art Collection North Rhine-Westphalia

When checking this organisation chart and considering what needs to be changed for a virtual museum, one realises that not much needs to be changed at all! However, it is assumed that this is a museum with a large collection, a high level of public impact, a high profile in the art world and international contacts. And a museum with a flexible form of sponsorship or organisation. It can be assumed that in a virtual museum, the tasks in the area of marketing in the broader sense (see Günter/Hausmann 2012 and Günter/Römhild 2023) and thus communication, interaction and participation are given a higher priority and are placed "higher" in organisational terms.

One recommendation would be for the management team of such a museum to be led by three people:

- Content management
- Technical IT management
- Financial management

Theatres are probably a good example of this, as in many cases they have organised these management divisions in this way because the areas of work are too specific to be left in one hand.

The collection, exhibition and restoration of media art objects, if they are available in our own collection, would be necessary as task-related positions. However, the latter position would actually be located in the IT department. This should only serve as an example of the fact that in administration, distribution, communication and mediation, the positions of analogue institutions are similar, but with different tasks.

Only the building, maintenance and property management aspect will be omitted. As this is usually a significant cost factor, its elimination will reduce costs. An element for pest prevention and eradication appears in a similar form in virtual museums as virus protection.

An important area of work is sales, combined with communication and mediation, as well as the financing requirements described elsewhere in the guide. There is a considerably greater need for input here.

15.2 Communication and marketing
(REINHARD GRÖNE)

The decision to use the internet as "venue" and the location of the museum has a direct influence on marketing and the associated communication. This is because, in principle, all those interested in the museum theme around the world are addressed. Thanks to various translation programmes, they can and want to be reached in all possible languages. This is an unrivalled advantage from the point of view of users and all other stakeholders. But also an unimaginable challenge. After all, cultural boundaries still need to be respected and observed. Faiths and religions often stand in the way of the same message in words and images.

All marketing-driven communication ultimately serves one goal: "sales" and acceptance by target groups, especially customer loyalty. On the one hand, it is an investment to increase visibility, acceptance, customer loyalty and "community building" – and thus to promote user numbers and user frequency. On the other hand, in the case of paid use, it serves to secure sustainable financing – albeit without the intention of making a profit.

Effective and efficient communication is not possible without a strong brand, without a "brand" that is as self-explanatory as possible. The focus will be on international appeal with a "wow effect". In addition to the visual logo, an acoustic logo also makes sense – especially in a medium that provides both as standard. The whole world is a target and doesn't just want to be invited, it wants to be "attracted" – no trivial task in the 24/7 communication jungle of the internet and the future *metaverse*. Social media campaigns and educational webinars – also live – take centre stage. The entire spectrum of classic communication supports the brand presence if it always leads directly to the digital offer: QR codes, links to the website, newsletter, community, museum shop.

Hybrid experience ability and supplementing the virtual presentation with a time-limited "pop-up museum" suggests itself as an additional customer loyalty programme.

Social media is the key to gaining leads and visitors. Customer loyalty can and should also go hand in hand with community building – from a global "circle of friends" to sponsors and partners interested in the target group.

15.3 The revenue model: B-to-C and B-to-B (REINHARD GRÖNE AND BERND GÜNTER)

For the "virtual museum" business model, the decision in favour of a revenue model may be existential. A distinction must be made as to which revenues should be sought from which target groups, i. e. fees from a business with consumers (end users) in the B-to-C relationship (business to consumer) and/or fees from relationships with institutions and companies in the B-to-B business (business to business).

Which B-to-C and which B-to-B revenues are conceivable?
It is likely that a broad audience of cultural consumers will be granted access and use free of charge. However, "admission" can be charged for special exhibitions, especially for high-interest or special-interest target groups. It is possible that the best way to generate revenue is through educational programmes (as part of the educational mission)

In addition, participation in special individual events and competitions can be linked to participation fees. In principle, models such as "Pay As You Stay" or "Pay What You Want" are also conceivable, with all the associated economic uncertainties.

An online museum shop – which, as in the offline world, can also be rented/leased to a suitable operator – can offer everything that an offline museum shop could offer: From catalogues in electronic form and printed catalogues (with shipping) to sending digital messages or greetings from the virtual museum. All merchandising objects with the museum brand, but also with exhibits including virtual gadgets such as NFTs, are suitable. Digital technology offers fast personalisation and individualisation for merchandising, where desired. The shop can also be used to offer offline experiences around the theme of the virtual museum for home use as paid webinars – e. g. webinars with curators and special virtual tours, but also encounters with the exhibits themselves (example: lending exhibits for a limited time for a fee, insurance and shipping costs).

In B-to-B relationships, institutional (organisational) target groups can be recruited as sponsoring partners – for a fee, of course, or through sponsoring in kind, personnel or expertise. Financially effective, time-limited off-line appearances of the virtual museum at interested partners' or sponsors' premises are conceivable – a temporary *pop-up museum* that can be "rented" as an attraction in its own right. A pop-up museum of this kind helps with visibility and community building and is also a suitable marketing and refinancing tool. The pop-up museum is a revenue-generating event in its own right with numerous opportunities for cooperation, just as with any face-to-face event. In such cooperative forms, revenue sharing, fees for the brand presence of cooperation partners, stand rental and admission fees can also be agreed.

A pop-up museum can also be licensed as a whole to one or more "operators", possibly for a limited period of time. The usual regulations and agreements for such events must be observed.

In the B-to-B business, it is also possible to support exhibitions and departments by mentioning the name of the sponsor, as is also practised by cultural institutions in the offline world. In the virtual world, a direct link to the partner's or sponsor's website is conceivable and realisable – with special guided tours for employees or customers. However, the link can also be made from the partner or sponsor to the virtual museum as a centre of excellence. External support can also be provided by bringing in virtual or digitised exhibits. "Loans", so to speak – either on a temporary or unlimited basis.

In principle, all options that a classic offline museum uses should be considered, provided they are adapted to the online world in a practical manner. Possibilities that can contribute to the balanced financing of the museum and, if necessary, supplement public and/or private funding and utilise the potential interest of B-to-B partners in a virtual museum are, for example

- Supply of information, material and "loans" on the subject of the virtual museum
- Sponsorship – formal, with contract (financial sponsorship, sponsorship in kind, know-how sponsorship, less: personnel sponsorship)
- Self-presentation, brand awareness, presence when named
- Advertising medium: can be changed at short notice, new target groups
- Market research surveys with quick results
- Renting a room in the virtual museum
- If necessary, support from the virtual museum for start-ups on museum-related topics.

15.4 Cost management and controlling

(OTMAR BÖHMER)

As part of the controlling required for business management, the question arises as to how the start-up phase of a virtual museum should be managed financially. This question of financing is crucially dependent on the question of the organisational form, the sponsorship.

- Is the virtual museum a predominantly commercially active, yet non-profit museum?
- Is the collection available?
- Does it have to be purchased at least in part?
- Do you co-operate with third parties at the start?
- Is there any capital/assets?

As with a start-up, the process leading up to the start of digital museum operations will require an introductory phase that must be financed. Technical and personnel investments are essential.

In day-to-day operations, target-oriented controlling is then required as a cross-functional management support system that collects the data required for corporate management, opens up information pools, channels information and summarises the data obtained in a recipient-oriented report that contains all decision-relevant data in a condensed form. Controlling is also responsible for setting targets, tracking targets and, if necessary, analysing deviations.

This definition shows that controlling is a service instrument for achieving a given goal. Defining the objective is particularly problematic in the cultural sector with regard to the quality of content and the presentation of artistic objectives. Before introducing controlling, care should be taken to ensure that the organisation has an explicitly formulated objective.

Financial accounting is available as a source of information, the data from which can be used to manage the projects and the institution. It is there, that knowledge about the internal status is available, which also provides a basis for discussion about future projects and perspectives for the sponsor and the supervisory bodies.

The instruments of strategic management include mission statements, visitor research and target agreements with the organisation and internal departments. Of these instruments, visitor research, appears to be a strongly results-oriented element due to its concretisation of requirements and objectives.

Controlling is first and foremost a tool for the management level of an institution to critically and permanently reflect on its own decisions.

In the further course, key figures can provide reference points for benchmarking with comparable competitors and providers.

Examples of statistical key figures:

- Total number of visitors (the conditions under which a user is considered a digital visitor must be clarified)
- Number of events
- Number of participants in events
- Number of guided tours
- Number of participants in guided tours
- Total exhibition key figures
- Costs and "Contribution margin 1"[1] per visitor
- Revenue/visitors
- Participants/event

1 In cost and activity accounting, "contribution margin 1" refers to the gross profit that is generated after deducting the direct costs of a cost unit (in other cost accounting objectives: the variable costs) from the revenue (price) of a product or object.

- % participants in events/visitors
- Participants in guided tours/guided tours
- % participants in guided tours/visitors
- Number of scientific publications
- Number of published media
- Circulation of published media
- Number of partners
- Number, status and volume of sponsors and supporters
- Feedback figures.

The financial planning and thus the financial controlling of a virtual museum will certainly have to be seen as a mixture of funding, sponsorship and self-generated income.

YASMIN MAHMOUDI

16. LEGAL ASPECTS

16.1 Intellectual property and copyright

For virtual museums, the question arises in particular as to whether a copyright licence is required for the virtual exhibition of the exhibits. Copyright grants the owner the exclusive right to use the work. This right arises automatically with the creation of a copyright work and does not expire until 70 years after the death of the creator. In principle, therefore, any use requires the permission of the copyright holder in the form of a licence. The German Copyright Act provides for exceptions to this principle, particularly for science and institutions such as museums. The law distinguishes between museums that do not pursue direct or indirect commercial purposes and publicly accessible museums that pursue commercial purposes. The latter are only permitted to reproduce without a licence for the purpose of preserving a work. In the case of non-commercial museums, the law also allows a work from the museum's collection or exhibition to be reproduced for the purposes of making it accessible, indexing, cataloguing, preserving and restoring it, even several times and with technical modifications. A further legal exception applies to so-called orphan works. These may be both reproduced and made publicly accessible. Orphan works are works from collections of publicly accessible museums if the contents of these collections have already been published and the rightholder could not be identified or located even after careful research. While the latter provision for orphan works expressly includes making content available to the public, i. e. uploading it to the internet, this does not apply to the previously described freedom of catalogue images. This only allows the reproduction, i. e. the making of a copy, but not the making available to the public. In summary, a virtual museum may therefore exhibit orphan works digitally without obtaining a licence, but not other copyright-protected works from its own collection or exhibition. In this respect, a licence is required for use on the Internet.

Virtual museums may exhibit all exhibits for which the copyright has expired due to the passage of time without obtaining a licence in advance. It is also permitted to exhibit works that are considered worthy of exhibition by the art market but lack the level of creativity required for copyright protection. One example is objet trouvée. If the virtual museums are not art museums, copyright plays a subordinate role. The level of creativity can be achieved in the design sector. Architectural sketches are also protected by copyright. Other exhibits, such as those from the field of natural history or local history, are generally not subject to copyright. If there is any doubt as to whether the level of creativity has been reached, a specialist lawyer should be consulted.

It must be checked whether a design patent or design right has been registered for the exhibit. Any trade mark rights must also be checked. Trade mark law differs from other intellectual property rights in that trade mark protection exists indefinitely. The trade mark "Meissen", for example, has been continuously protected under trade mark law for over 500 years. If a trade mark is protected, this does not automatically mean that it can only be displayed with the permission of the rights holder. In principle, so-called exhaustion occurs with the sale of a product. This means that the trade mark owner cannot prohibit the exhibition of their products in a museum. This may be different in the case of a virtual exhibition if, for example, the exhibition transfers the image of the branded product. If branded products or products whose design is protected are to be exhibited virtually, it is advisable to consult a specialist intellectual property lawyer beforehand. Obtaining legal advice can always be omitted if you have the express authorisation of the rights holder in text form. The text form is intended to ensure that the authorisation obtained can be proven. This is not only relevant in the event of a dispute, but also when the natural persons involved change.

16.2 Image rights

Image rights are of great practical relevance for every virtual museum. Regardless of whether the virtually displayed exhibit itself enjoys copyright protection, the person who photographed or filmed the exhibit is entitled to image rights. Furthermore, the photographer is generally entitled to be named. This also applies to the person who recorded the video or reel. Here, the virtual museum should ensure that the relevant image rights have been obtained for each individual exhibit, ideally including the right to edit and sub-licence. The right to sub-licence facilitates any loans. Obtaining the image rights is often overlooked in practice if the images were supposedly created in-house. As the museum is rarely run in the form of a partnership or by a natural person as the owner, it is likely to be persons who have created images in fulfilment of their obligations arising from an employment or service relationship. In this case in particular, it remains the case that the image rights must be expressly obtained, unless the employment or service relationship stipulates otherwise. In this case, it is advisable to make an express provision stating that the rights to the images or videos of the exhibits belong to the museum. A corresponding regulation is also required in particular if the images were taken by a volunteer employee.

The image rights must always be clarified, regardless of the subject of the image and the type of collection, i. e. in the case of a technology museum or other museum outside the art sector.

If the image rights are held by the museum, as recommended above, it can also pass them on to third parties, for example in the context of loans. Furthermore, licences can be commissioned to distribute posters or postcards of museum exhibits. For NFTs, see 16.3 below. It should always be noted that the rights of both the photographer and the artist must be obtained. Depending on the legal form of the museum's sponsoring company, it must be ensured that the maximum taxable amounts for a commercial operation are not exceeded.

16.3 AI art

In the legal assessment of artificial intelligence (AI), a distinction must be made between the different phases of the use of AI.

The first step is to train the AI by entering content, some of which is protected by copyright. This is often done automatically through *scraping*. While artists in the USA are already taking legal action against the use of their content as training data for AI, the legal situation in Germany is governed by Section 44b of the German Copyright Act (UrhG): The automated analysis and reproduction of lawfully accessible works for text and data mining is generally lawful if no *opt-out* has been given. No permission needs to be obtained from the copyright holder for text and data mining and this type of use does not trigger a licence obligation. However, the reproductions must be deleted if they are no longer required for text and data mining. Copyright holders, however, have the option of prohibiting this use of their copyrighted works in the form of an *opt-out*. However, the reservation only applies to works that are lawfully accessible online if it is machine-readable and has no retroactive effect. The deletion obligation has the disadvantage for users of text and data mining, especially in the scientific field, that the scientific knowledge gained cannot be verified because the source data must be deleted. This is taken into account by Section 60d UrhG, which permits reproductions for scientific research if neither own commercial purposes are pursued nor if there is cooperation with a private company that has a decisive influence on the research organisation and preferential access to its scientific results.

This privilege also expressly applies to publicly accessible museums if they do not pursue commercial purposes.

In a second step, the question arises as to the legal assessment of the use of AI to generate a result. In particular, this raises the question of the copyright protection of *prompts*, i. e. the short input texts with which the AI is prompted to generate corresponding content. Such *prompts generally* do not reach the required level of creativity. Just as the client of a portrait does not become a co-author because he gives the artist precise specifications such as format, posture, colour or deviations in favour of a more visually appealing result, the person who triggers the AI by means of a *prompt is* not the author of the result generated by the AI.

The virtual museum is generally allowed to exhibit AI. For example, the AI painting "Edmond de Belamy", which was sold for USD 432,500.00 at Christie's auction house in 2018, is in the public domain despite its success on the market, as it cannot be attributed to a human creator as a work of computer algorithm or artificial intelligence. In the absence of copyright, there is no right to attribution, nor do third parties have to obtain a licence if they want to copy, publish or otherwise use the work commercially. However, caution is advised here. Even if there are no copyrights to the content generated by AI, not everything that is created with the help of a computer is free to use.

Conversely, not everything generated by AI is automatically legal. In particular, the output may infringe the personal rights of third parties. This is the responsibility of the museum that uses the corresponding output without legal scrutiny. One example of this is the supposed new hit by the two rappers Drake and The Weekend, which was generated by AI without their involvement or consent.

Another example is the topic of NFTs (non-fungible tokens). The decisive factor is that the NFT itself is merely a digital character string and not the asset it represents. The NFT is therefore more of a crypto security. The NFT itself is a digital certificate for something outside the blockchain, whereby the value secured by the NFT is not fully stored in the blockchain even if it is a digital asset. An NFT is always divided into two parts; the token and what the token secures. In this respect, the reporting is highly simplified and misleading when supposed images of NFTs, such as the Beeple collage "Everydays – the first 5000 days" (2021), are shown and the purchase price of USD 69 million is mentioned. The image file is only linked to the NFT by means of an IPFS hash value. Rights of use to the linked digital artworks are also not automatically transferred to the purchaser of an NFT, but must be granted separately by contract.

If you consider the dichotomy between token and asset, it becomes clear that NFTs are not bringing anything completely new to the (art) market. Decades before the first NFT was coined, the sale of conceptual art was already a niche area of the art market in which the buyer received at best a certificate instead of a physical work, as in the case of Yves Klein's "Zones of Immaterial Pictorial Sensibility". Yves Klein issued receipts for his invisible works, which he had paid for in pure gold. Half of the gold was thrown into the Seine in the presence of the purchaser and the receipt was burnt at the same time.

What does this mean for the utilisation of copyright-protected content by a virtual museum in the form of NFTs? The question has not yet been conclusively clarified. There is some evidence to suggest that copyrights are not infringed by the minting of an NFT. However, in order to avoid time-consuming and costly legal disputes, it is advisable to only mint and exhibit works as NFTs where the consent of the potential rights holders has been obtained or no third-party rights are affected.

NFTs are not limited to digital content, but can also represent physical works. An example of the latter is the trend among some museums to mint popular crowd-pullers from their collections, such as the Belvedere in Vienna. Anyone can purchase a digital copy of Gustav Klimt's Kiss as an NFT. Fractionalisation combines the two aspects of NFT and *fractional ownership*. In this respect, minting your own NFTs offers a potential source of income for virtual museums.

The legal framework with regard to AI is not static. On March 13th 2024 the EU has already approved a regulation, the so-called AI Act. The following is planned with regard to generative AI such as Chat GPT, DALLE and Midjourney:

- transparency through a mandatory "AI-generated" notice and
- An obligation to make publicly available a detailed summary of the data subject to copyright that was used to train the respective AI.

The second transparency obligation in particular contradicts the current law on text and data mining outlined above.

16.4 Competition law

Competition law is relevant to the operation of a virtual museum in two respects. If and insofar as the virtual museum offers a museum shop, all regulations on buying and selling on the Internet must be observed. This includes the obligation to provide general terms and conditions as well as information on the right of cancellation. In the event that a newsletter is provided, the virtual museum must adhere to the double opt-in rule, as the sending of the newsletter would otherwise be legally categorised as spam.

A privacy policy, a proper legal notice and a reference to the online dispute resolution platform are also mandatory. Further information obligations arise from the distance selling regulations of the German Civil Code (BGB) and from the obligations in electronic business transactions also regulated in the BGB.

The virtual museum must also refrain from misleading commercial behaviour. One example would be inaccurate unique selling point advertising, for example advertising one of several virtual theatre museums as the supposedly only virtual theatre museum. Another example would be misleading information about a supposed authorisation by a renowned institution or person.

16.5 Media and press law

In addition to the aspects already mentioned, care must be taken to ensure that both editorial contributions to the virtual museum and other designs comply with media and press law regulations. It should be emphasised that links to third-party reporting are permitted. However, it is not permitted to upload a screenshot or a PDF file of a third-party article to your own website in order to report on the coverage of the virtual museum or an exhibition or event organised by the museum. Here too, permission must first be obtained. Often this will only be granted for a fee, especially by publishers. According to § 18 MSTV, the imprint of the virtual museum must always include a person responsible under press law in the form of a natural person with at least a full first name, surname and address if journalistic and editorial content is available.

16.6 Applicability of German law

Across all areas of law, all of the aforementioned aspects relate to German law. Within the European Union, the law is largely harmonised so that many regulations can be similar. Nevertheless, differences remain, particularly in copyright law. When examining which law applies to a digital offer on the Internet, the law is usually based on who the provider is addressing as intended. Decisive factors for this include the language version of the offer as well as where advertising is carried out, which top-level domain is used and where delivery is made in the case of an online shop.

16.7 Legal form of the operating company

The choice of legal form for a virtual museum depends largely on its sponsor. If the state is involved through the federal government, federal states or local authorities, a private-public partnership can be considered. For purely private sponsors, it depends on whether the museum should also make a profit. In this case, the establishment of a GmbH or a UG (limited liability company) is an option. If the focus is not on making a profit, the legal forms of a foundation, a non-profit limited liability company (gGmbH) or the establishment of a registered association should be considered. Which legal form makes sense depends, among other things, on the composition of the organisation and the available financial resources. In this respect, it is always advisable to consult a tax advisor in advance.

REINHARD GRÖNE

17. ANALOGUE AND DIGITAL

17.1 Virtual offers from and for "analogue" people

The first appearance, the "premiere" of a virtual museum can be an opening in the analogue world for reasons of publicity. A classic "push the red button" event. If possible, under prominent patronage, it will be an attention-grabbing and, above all, press-worthy photo event. With many invited guests, representatives of supporters and sponsors, with friends and sponsors.

Every virtual museum is always a bit "hybrid" because part of its infrastructure also remains part of the analogue world: Employees need workstations, the necessary technology ("hardware") from server to programming and control is located or created in the analogue world. This can be decentralised and distributed around the world and supported digitally as far as possible, but in the end, it is analogue people who keep the business "running". And for whom it is created and set up.

There is another reason why this "hybrid" character of the virtual museum will always be and remain a supplement to the essentially digital offering. Because the most important group of stakeholders for the success of a virtual museum offering, the visitors and users, are and will remain part of the "analogue world". That is where they live and that is where they want and need to be met. Even when they set off with their digital devices such as computers, tablets and/or head-mounted displays. Exciting experiences with augmented reality (AR), virtual reality and mixed reality (MR) make it possible to immerse yourself in a different, digitally generated and narrated reality. In the future "metaverse", it will also be the people of the offline world who send their avatars on a journey of discovery. The processing of the experience takes place in the minds sitting in front of or inside the digital devices.

The next step in digital networking with fellow human beings will be able to take place in this new virtual reality. This "Social VR" is the third development stage of the internet, usually referred to as "Web 3.0". In marketing terms, it is also heralded as the "metaverse" by various providers. Whatever this "metaverse" may ultimately look like, virtual museums will be an integral part of it: And 24/7 – always open and accessible worldwide.

17.2 "Pop-up museum": Visibility and community building

There will always be appearances of the virtual museum in the analogue world. Just as there are pop-up stores today, which sometimes appear in the most surprising places for only a short time, there will also be pop-up museums that serve the visibility and community building of interested users and visitors. If you like, you can bring "your" virtual museum into your home for your next birthday party. All you need is the right digital devices and the journey can begin.

Instead of "watching football" together on TV, a virtual playful visit to the museum can also be organised in an uncomplicated, comfortable and stimulating way.

BERND GÜNTER

18. EPILOGUE

As can be seen, virtual museums can fulfil all the tasks that the museum associations regard as constitutive. Virtual museums can cover topics and represent centres of competence for subjects for which museum or similar educational and entertainment institutions do not yet exist or find it difficult. Virtual museums can be accessed at any time and from any place. They provide access to people who are less able or willing to utilise other ways of accessing cultural assets. Virtual museums should not draw visitors away from analogue cultural institutions; rather, they should complement and expand the museum landscape according to current and future (technical) possibilities.

Disinterest or even resistance to the topic of "virtual museums" is understandable. But the digital prerequisites are there – and they are being further perfected. Digitisation has already taken hold in all areas of life. In terms of content, themes, formats and forms of presentation, there are virtually no limits to the imagination when it comes to designing virtual museums.

Virtual museums open up completely new circles of interest for the diverse "world of museums" and for the preservation of cultural assets. In line with the demands of national and international museum organisations.

SOURCES AND LITERATURE

Ahlert, Dieter, Backhaus, Klaus & Meffert, Heribert: Geschäftsmodelle im E-Business. MCM-Studie zum Deutschen Marketing-Tag 2001, in: *absatzwirtschaft. Sonderausgabe* October (2001), pp. 32–44.

ARt chat von nextmuseum.io.: **https://nextmuseum.io/experiments/art-chat/** [accessed 16.01.2023].

Bitkom e. V.: Klimaschutz durch digitale Technologien – Chancen und Risiken 2020. **https://www.bitkom.org/klimaschutz-digital** [accessed 27.08.2022].

Brandt, Mathias: Video-Streaming ist für 60 % des Traffics verantwortlich, **https://de.statista.com/infografik/21188/zusammensetzung-des-weltweiten-downstream-internet-traffics/** [accessed 26.08.2022].

Brüggemann, Anke: The trade-offs between digitalization and climate-action: Why digitalization must be sustainable, **https://www.kfw.de/PDF/Download-Center/Konzernthemen/Research/PDF-Dokumente-Fokus-Volkswirtschaft/Fokus-englische-Dateien/Fokus-2021-EN/Focus-No.-341-August-2021-Digitalisation-and-Climate.pdf** [accessed 28.08.2022].

Carius, Hendrikje & Fackler, Guido: Ausstellungen digital kuratieren. Formen und Diskurse, Herausforderungen und Chancen, in: Carius, Hendrikje & Fackler, Guido (Eds.): *Exponat – Raum – Interaktion. Perspektiven für das Kuratieren digitaler Ausstellungen*, Göttingen 2022, pp. 15–38.

Deeken, Michael & Fuchs, Tobias: *Agiles Management als Antwort auf die Herausforderungen der Digitalisierung*, Wiesbaden 2018.

Deutscher Museumsbund e. V. und Bundesverband Museumspädagogik e. V. (Hrsg): *Leitfaden Bildung und Vermittlung im Museum gestalten*, Berlin 2020.

Encyclopaedia Britannica (o. J.): virtual museum, **https://www.britannica.com/topic/virtual-museum** [accessed 19.12.2022].

European Commission – Joint Research Centre: *AI watch. Defining Artificial Intelligence 2.0. Towards an operational definition and taxonomy for the AI landscape*, Luxemburg 2021.

Falk, John H.: Understanding Museums Visitors' Motivations and Learning, in: Ida Brændholt Lundgaard & Jacob Thorek Jensen (Eds.): *Museums. Social Learning Spaces and Knowledge Producing Processes*, Kopenhagen 2013, pp. 106–127.

Gailhofer, Peter, Führ, Martin & Gröger, Jens: The European Parliament's amendments to the AI Act. A plausible approach for the „Ecological Alignment" of AI?, **https://www.oeko.de/news/pressemeldungen/kuenstliche-intelligenz-oekologisch-ausrichten/** [accessed 15.11.2023].

Geipel, Andrea & Hohmann, Georg: VR/AR – Digitale Räume im Museum, in: Mohr, Henning & Modarressi-Tehrani, Diana (Eds.): *Museen der Zukunft. Trends und Herausforderungen eines innovationsorientierten Kulturmanagements*, Bielefeld 2021, pp. 257–273.

Günter, Bernd: Verlässlichkeit als Wettbewerbsvorteil im Business-to-Business-Marketing, in: Büschken, Joachim, Voeth, Markus & Weiber, Rolf (Eds.): *Innovationen für das Industriegütermarketing*, Stuttgart 2007, pp. 185–199.

Günter, Bernd & Hausmann, Andrea: *Kulturmarketing*, 2. Ed., Wiesbaden 2012.

Günter, Bernd: Virtuelle Museen – Zukunftsmusik oder reale Option? in: *KulturBetrieb*, Issue 4, October 2016, pp. 10–11.

Günter, Bernd: Virtual Reality und der Weg zum virtuellen Museum. Illusion, Chance oder gar Notwendigkeit?, in: Emmert, Claudia & Neddermeyer, Ida (Eds.): *Schöne neue Welten. Tagungsband zur Abschlusstagung April 2018*, Zeppelin-Museum Friedrichshafen 2019, pp. 220–231.

Günter, Bernd & Römhild, Julia: *Marketing für Kunst und Kultur*, Volume 1, Stuttgart 2023.

Gröger, Jens & Liu, Ran et al.: Green Cloud Computing. Lebenszyklusbasierte Datenerhebung zu Umweltwirkungen des Cloud Computing, **https://www.umweltbundesamt.de/publikationen/green-cloud-computing** [accessed 14.01.2024].

Gröger, Jens & Liu, Ran et al.: Umweltzeichen Blauer Engel für Server und Datenspeicherprodukte https://www.umweltbundesamt.de/publikationen/umweltzeichen-blauer-engel-fuer-server [accessed 14.01.2024].

Hahn, Hans Peter: Das digitalisierte Museum – Erweiterung oder Transformation? Zur Selbstpositionierung von Museen im 21. Jahrhundert, in: Udo Andraschke & Sarah Wagner (Eds.): *Objekte im Netz*, Bielefeld 2020, pp. 45–67.

Hahn, Rüdiger: *Sustainability Management: Global Perspectives on Concepts, Instruments, and Stakeholders*, Fellbach 2022.

Hermon, Sorin & Hazan, Susan: Rethinking the virtual museum, in: Institute of Electrical and Electronics Engineers (Eds.): *Digital Heritage International Congress (DigitalHeritage)*, Volume 2 (2013), pp. 625–632.

Hessische Staatskanzlei: Studie zu Nachhaltigkeitspotenzialen in und durch Digitalisierung in Hessen, **https://digitales.hessen.de/starke-netze/recheninfrastrukturen/nachhaltigkeit** [accessed 28.08.2022].

High-Level Expert Group on Artifical Intelligence by the European Commission: A Definition of AI: Main Capabilities and Disciplines, **ec.europa.eu/newsroom/dae/document.cfm?doc_id=56341** [accessed 08.12.2023].

Homburg, Christian: *Marketingmanagement: Strategie-Instrumente-Umsetzung-Unternehmensführung*, Wiesbaden 2020.

Höge, Holger: Rezeptionsverhalten der Ausstellungsgäste, in: Walz, Markus (Eds.): *Handbuch Museum. Geschichte, Aufgaben, Perspektiven*, Stuttgart 2016, pp. 270–273.

ICOM – Conseil international des musées: *Ethische Richtlinien für Museen von ICOM*, Berlin 2010.

ICOM: ICOM approves a new museum definition, **https://icom.museum/en/news/icom-approves-a-new-museum-definition/** [accessed 19.12.2022].

Klinke, Harald: Smart Museum. Cultural Heritage in the Virtual Space, **https://medium.com/@HxxxKxxx/smart-museum-cultural-heritage-in-the-virtual-space-fdc720e4650a** [accessed 30.01.2023].

Knaus, Gudrun: *Leitfaden für digitales Sammlungsmanagement an Kunstmuseen*, Heidelberg 2019.

Köhne, Eckart: Betriebssystem Museum (Editorial), in: *Museumskunde*, Band 83 (2019), Berlin, pp. 1.

Lange, Steffen & Santarius, Tilman: *Smarte Grüne Welt. Digitalisierung zwischen Überwachung, Konsum und Nachhaltigkeit*, München 2018.

Meffert, Heribert, Burmann, Christoph & Kirchgeorg, Manfred: *Marketing: Grundlagen marktorientierter Unternehmensführung. Konzepte – Instrumente – Praxisbeispiele*, 13. Auflage, Wiesbaden 2019.

Mohr, Henning & Modarressi-Tehrani, Diana: Museen der Zukunft: Trends und Herausforderungen eines innovationsorientierten Kulturmanagements, in: Mohr, Henning & Modarressi-Tehrani, Diana (Eds.). *Museen der Zukunft: Trends und Herausforderungen eines innovationsorientierten Kulturmanagements*, Bielefeld 2021, pp. 9–24.

Mörsch, Carmen: *Zeit für Vermittlung. Eine Online-Publikation zur Kunstvermittlung*, Zürich 2012.

Niewerth, Dennis: *Dinge – Nutzer – Netze. Von der Virtualisierung des Musealen zur Musealisierung des Virtuellen*, Bielefeld 2018.

Niewerth, Dennis: Virtuelle Museen, in: Kasprowicz, Dawid & Rieger, Stefan (Eds.): *Handbuch Virtualität*, Wiesbaden 2020, pp. 521–532.

Polycarpou, Christiana: The VIMM Definition of a Virtual Museum, **https://www.vi-mm.eu/2018/01/10/the-vimm-definition-of-a-virtual-museum/** [accessed 14.01.2024].

Pöllmann, Lorenz & Herrmann, Clara: *Der digitale Kulturbetrieb. Strategien, Handlungsfelder und Best Practices des digitalen Kulturmanagements*, Wiesbaden 2019.

Preuß, Kristine & Hofmann, Fabian: Einleitung, in: Preuß, Kristine & Hofmann, Fabian (Eds.): *Kunstvermittlung im Museum. Ein Erfahrungsraum*, Münster 2017, pp. 11–27.

PwC Deutschland: Deutscher Virtual-Reality-Markt wächst über die Nische hinaus, **https://www.pwc.de/de/technologie-medien-und-telekommunikation/studie-deutscher-virtual-reality-markt-waechst-ueber-die-nische-hinaus.html** [accessed 29.07.2022].

Villaespesa, Elena & Murphy, Oonagh (Eds.): *Künstliche Intelligenz und Museen – Ein Toolkit*, London 2022.

Römhild, Julia & Heinzelmann, Rebecca: Nachhaltigkeit als kulturelle Herausforderung – Die Rolle von Museen im Kontext Nachhaltiger Entwicklung, in: Hilgers-Sekowsky, Julia, Richter, Nicole & Ermel, Nicole (Eds.): *Nachhaltigkeit in Nonprofit-Organisationen Transdisziplinäre Perspektiven für ein zukunftsfähiges Management*, Wiesbaden 2023, pp. 151–171.

Schößler, Tom: Ein neues Preismodell für Museen im Praxistest. Pay As You Stay – Zahl, solange Du bleibst, **https://www.kulturmanagement.net/Themen/Ein-neues-Preismodell-fuer-Museen-im-Praxistest-Pay-As-You-Stay-Zahl-solange-Du-bleibst,4100** [accessed 26.08.2022].

Schreyögg, Georg & Koch, Jochen: *Management: Grundlagen der Unternehmensführung*, Wiesbaden 2020.

Schweibenz, Werner: Das virtuelle Museum. Überlegungen zum Begriff und Wesen des Museums im Internet, **https://mai-tagung.lvr.de/media/mai_tagung/pdf/2001/schweibenz.pdf** [accessed 19.12.2022].

Schweibenz, Werner: *Vom traditionellen Museum zum virtuellen Museum*, Frankfurt am Main 2008.

Schweibenz, Werner: Virtuelle Museen, in: Walz, Markus (Eds.): *Handbuch Museum*, Stuttgart 2016, pp. 198–200.

Schweibenz, Werner: The virtual museum: an overview of its origins, concepts, and terminology, in: *The Museum Review*, Vol. 4 Nr. 1 (2019), pp. 1–29.

Statista: Prognose zum weltweiten Umsatz mit Virtual Reality bis 2025, **https://de.statista.com/statistik/daten/studie/318536/umfrage/prognose-zum-umsatz-mit-virtual-reality-weltweit/** [accessed 29.07.2022].

Stender, Christine & Stärk, Theresa: Art 4.0 Toolbox, Projekt Curriculum 4.0 NRW – Digitale Kunstvermittlung | ART 4.0, Laufzeit 2021–2022, **https://www.kuk.hhu.de/curriculum-40-nrw-digitale-kunstvermittlung-art-40** [accessed 14.01.2024].

Team Z museum4punkt0: Perspektive nachhaltige Nachnutzung: Vernetzung für die digitale Vermittlung, **https://www.museum4punkt0.de/perspektive-nachhaltige-nachnutzung-vernetzung-fuer-die-digitale-vermittlung/** [accessed 26.08.2022].

Thiel, Sonja & Bernhardt, Johannes C.: *AI in Museums: Reflections, Perspectives and Applications*, Bielefeld 2023.

Umweltbundesamt (UBA) (Eds.)/Gröger, J./Liu, R. et al. (2021), Green Cloud Computing Lebenszyklusbasierte Datenerhebung zu Umweltwirkungen des Cloud Computing. Abschlussbericht, **http://www.umweltbundesamt.de/publikationen** (Stand 27.08.2022).

Wissenschaftlicher Beirat der Bundesregierung Globale Umweltveränderungen: Unsere gemeinsame digitale Zukunft. Zusammenfassung, **https://www.wbgu.de/fileadmin/user_upload/wbgu/publikationen/hauptgutachten/hg2019/pdf/WBGU_HGD2019_Z.pdf** [accessed 24.01.2023].

Virtual Museum Transnational Network: **www.v-must.net** [accessed 20.01.2023].

Zouboula, Nikoletta & Fokides, Emmanuel et al.: Virtual Reality and Museum. An Educational Application for Museum Education, in: *International Journal of Emerging Technologies in Learning*, Bd. 3 (2008), pp. 89–95.

CONTRIBUTORS

In August 2024, the author group "Forum Virtuelle Museen" consists of the following personalities:

Isabelle Becker supports all press and communication activities of the Art Basel as part of the communication team for the art fairs for modern and contemporary art in Basel, Miami Beach, Hong Kong, and Paris. Her main place of work is Basel, Switzerland. She completed her master's degree in Art Mediation and Cultural Management at Heinrich Heine University, Düsseldorf. She also holds a double bachelor's degree in Business Administration and studied in Lörrach and Treforest (Wales).

Otmar Böhmer is the executive director of the Volkswagen Art Foundation and managing director of the Kunstmuseum Wolfsburg.

Reinhard Gröne is the founder and executive director of the business angel-network ANGEL ENGINE e.V. His focus is on innovations and startups in the culture and creative industries. He is involved in various companies and projects.

Bernd Günter is the former holder of the Chair of Business Administration, especially Marketing, at Heinrich Heine University, Düsseldorf. He is currently a lecturer in the master's program in Art Mediation and Cultural Management at HHU.

Rebecca Heinzelmann is a cultural manager and mediator (M.A.). Currently, she works as a sustainability manager, supporting cultural institutions in developing comprehensive sustainability strategies and guiding processes towards management systems (e.g., ISO 20121, EMAS) and measurement tools (e.g., CO2 balances). She completed her master's degree in Art Mediation and Cultural Management at Heinrich Heine University, Düsseldorf.

Anja Kircher-Kannemann is a PhD historian. She currently works as a curator and collection manager at the Jugendstilforum Bad Nauheim. She also supervises various digital history communication projects for the city of Bad Nauheim. She has been running the blog Kultur-Geschichte(n)-Digital on topics of digital culture and history communication for several years.

Yasmin Mahmoudi started her legal career at Clifford Chance LLP and then founded the law firm Dr. Mahmoudi & Partner Rechtsanwälte mbB. She is a specialist lawyer for industrial property rights, arbitrator at the Court of Arbitration for Art, and lecturer at Heinrich Heine University Düsseldorf for legal foundations of art and cultural management.

Julia Römhild is an academic councilor for cultural management at Heinrich Heine University Düsseldorf and coordinates and teaches in the master's program in Art Mediation and Cultural Management. In her current research, she focuses particularly on consumer behavior, strategic marketing, as well as cultural marketing and management.

Holger Simon is an art historian and entrepreneur. He is the initiator of pioneering digital projects such as the prometheus image archive (2001), the Digital Historical Archive Cologne (2009), and the consortium NFDI4Culture (2020). With his company Pausanio, he advises cultural and memory institutions on digital transformation and accompanies them through change processes. In 2013, he founded the Pausanio Academy as a training center for people in art, culture, and science.

Theresa Stärk is a research assistant at the Institute of Art History at Heinrich Heine University Düsseldorf. Her research focuses on digital art mediation, aesthetic experience in virtual space, and digital museum audience research. She completed her master's degree in Art Mediation and Cultural Management at Heinrich Heine University, Düsseldorf.

Laura Zebisch is currently working at the Goethe-Institut. There she is responsible for organizational development, with a particular focus on strategic sustainability management. She completed her master's degree in Art Mediation and Cultural Management at Heinrich Heine University, Düsseldorf.

With the assistance of Anne Seebeck and Karl-Ludwig Döring.

IMAGE CREDITS

Figure 1, p. 44, figure 2, p. 50, figure 3, p. 51, figure 5, p. 79: own illustrations; figure 4, p. 55: Gudrun Knaus, Guidelines for digital collection management at art museums, Heidelberg 2019, p. 19.